Intellectual Property Infringement Damages

SUBSCRIPTION NOTICE

This Wiley product is updated on a periodic basis with supplements to reflect important changes in the subject matter. If you purchased this product directly from John Wiley & Sons, Inc., we have already recorded your subscription for this update service.

If, however, you purchased this product from a bookstore and wish to receive (1) the current update at no additional charge, and (2) future updates and revised or related volumes billed separately with a 30-day examination review, please send your name, company name (if applicable), address, and the title of the product to:

> Supplement Department
> John Wiley & Sons, Inc.
> One Wiley Drive
> Somerset, NJ 08875
> 1-800-225-5945

For customers outside the United States, please contact the Wiley office nearest you:

Professional & Reference Division
John Wiley & Sons Canada, Ltd.
22 Worcester Road
Rexdale, Ontario M9W 1L1
CANADA
(416) 675-3580
1-800-567-4797
FAX (416) 675-6599

John Wiley & Sons, Ltd.
Baffins Lane
Chichester
West Sussex, PO19 1UD
UNITED KINGDOM
(44) (243) 779777

Jacaranda Wiley Ltd.
PRT Division
P.O. Box 174
North Ryde, NSW 2113
AUSTRALIA
(02) 805-1100
FAX (02) 805-1597

John Wiley & Sons (SEA) Pte. Ltd.
37 Jalan Pemimpin
Block B #05-04
Union Industrial Building
SINGAPORE 2057
(65) 258-1157

Intellectual Property Infringement Damages
A Litigation Support Handbook

SECOND EDITION

Russell L. Parr

WILEY

JOHN WILEY & SONS, INC.

New York • Chichester • Weinheim • Brisbane • Toronto • Singapore

Published simultaneously in Canada.

This publication is designed to provide accurate and authoritative information in regard to the subject matter covered. It is sold with the understanding that the publisher is not engaged in rendering legal, accounting, or other professional services. If legal advice or other expert assistance is required, the services of a competent professional person should be sought.

Library of Congress Cataloging-in-Publication Data:

Parr, Russell L.
    Intellectual property infringement damages : a litigation support
handbook / Russell L. Parr.—2nd ed.
        p.   cm.
    Includes bibliographical references and index.
    ISBN 0-471-32015-3 (cloth : alk. paper)
    1. Intellectual property—United States.   2. Damages—United
States.   I. Title.
KF2979.P36   1999
346.7304'8—dc21   98-47985
                                                           CIP

Printed in the United States of America.

10 9 8 7 6 5 4 3 2 1

About the Author

Russell L. Parr, CFA, ASA is Senior Vice President of AUS Consultants. He is an expert in determining the value of intellectual property and has written many books including the co-authoring of *Valuation of Intellectual Property and Intangible*, published by John Wiley & Sons, New York. He is also President of Intellectual Property Research Associates, a company that publishes various books about licensing agreements and royalty rates involving patents, trademarks, and copyrights.

Mr. Parr is responsible for the completion of complex consulting assignments involving the valuation and pricing of patents, trademarks, copyrights, and other intangible assets. His opinions are used to accomplish licensing transactions, mergers, acquisitions, tax-related transfer pricing, litigation support, collateral-based financing, and joint ventures. Mr. Parr also conducts customized research into industry-specific factors that drive royalty rates.

Mr. Parr is publisher of the highly respected *Licensing Economics Review*, which reports detailed information about the economic aspects of intellectual property licensing and joint venturing. Since September 1990, he has published royalty rate information from around the world and discussed patent and trademark infringement decisions.

Recent assignments of Mr. Parr's have included the valuation of the Dr. Seuss copyrights. He has also completed valuation and royalty rate studies for communications technology, pharmaceuticals, semiconductor process technology, automotive battery technology, lasers, agricultural technology, biotechnology, computer software, drug delivery systems, medical products technology, consumer electronics, incinerator feed systems, camera technology, flowers, trademarks, motivational book copyrights, and cosmetics.

One of the books that Mr. Parr co-authored with Gordon V. Smith, *Intellectual Property: Licensing and Joint Venture Profit Strategies*, is listed as a Publication Resource on the Web page of the National Institute of Standards and Technology, Advanced Technology Program of the U.S. Department of Commerce. Another book that Mr. Parr co-authored with Mr. Smith, *Valuation of Intellectual Property & Intangible Assets, First Edition*, has been designated as an Authoritative Reference by the Business Valuation Committee of The American Society of Appraisers, 1991.

Mr. Parr's education includes a Masters in Business Administration, Rutgers University, 1981; a Bachelor of Science in Electrical Engineering, Rutgers University, 1976. He also holds the Chartered Financial Analyst (CFA) designation from the Association of Investment Management and Research, 1986; and the Accredited Senior Appraiser (ASA) designation from The American Society of Appraisers, 1986.

Books that Mr. Parr has authored or co-authored are listed below:

Royalty Rates for Technology, Yardley, Pennsylvania: Intellectual Property Research Associates, 1997.

The Royalty Rate Report for Pharmaceuticals & Biotechnology, Third Edition, Yardley, Pennsylvania: Intellectual Property Research Associates, 1996.

Royalty Rates for Trademarks & Copyrights, Yardley, Pennsylvania: Intellectual Property Research Associates, 1998.

Technology Licensing—Corporate Strategies for Maximizing Value, co-author, New York: John Wiley & Sons, 1996.

Valuation of Intellectual Property and Intangible Assets, co-author, New York: John Wiley & Sons, 1990.

Valuation of Intellectual Property and Intangible Assets, Second Edition, annually supplemented, co-author, New York: John Wiley & Sons, 1994. Translated into Japanese and published in Japan, 1996.

Investing In Intangible Assets: Finding and Profiting From Hidden Corporate Value, New York: John Wiley & Sons, 1991.

Intellectual Property: Licensing and Joint Venture Profit Strategies, Second Edition, co-authored, annually supplemented, co-author, New York: John Wiley & Sons, 1998.

Mr. Parr can be reached at AUS Consultants, 1004 Buckingham Way, Yardley, Pennsylvania 19067 USA.

Preface

This book continues to represent a guide for establishing damages where intellectual property has been infringed. It combines past methods of damage analysis with advanced theories that are based on investment rate of return analysis. This new edition has been greatly improved by the contributions of Richard J. Gering, Ph.D. Director, Pricewater-houseCoopers, LLP and Gordon V. Smith, President of AUS Consultants. Dr. Gering has expanded and greatly enhanced the discussion of Lost Profits and insightfully analyzed recent court decisions. Mr. Smith has brilliantly brought organization to the challenging and sometimes contradictory question of trademark damages analysis. In addition to these new chapters, I have completely reorganized the presentation of material into a more logical flow.

Another subtle change in this edition involves a reduction of legal definitions and examples of intellectual property. Many excellent texts address these aspects of intellectual property. My purpose for this book is a more focused effort about a unique niche of intellectual property. As such, I have assumed that readers have a good understanding about the nature of intellectual property.

My purpose in writing this book is to provide a comprehensive tool for those that are engaged in the enormous struggle of intellectual property infringement damages. I say the struggle is enormous because the importance of intellectual property has eclipsed all other assets, and damage awards can destroy the corporations that lose these lawsuits. My hope in writing this book is to somehow inspire those that are involved in infringement lawsuits to settle their disputes.

Russell L. Parr
Yardley, Pennsylvania

Acknowledgments

This new edition has been greatly enhanced by two very important people, Gordon V. Smith and Richard J. Gering.

GORDON V. SMITH is president of AUS Consultants in Morristown, NJ, and a leader of intellectual property valuation. This book has greatly benefited from his chapter about trademarks. Mr. Smith's clients include a prestigious collection of multinational corporations for which he provides intellectual property consulting services. In addition to his many books, he actively speaks at conferences around the world. Most recently he was invited to speak in China and Argentina. Mr. Smith is an active member of the International Trademark Association and the Licensing Executive Society. He is also a founder of the Intellectual Property Management Institute and is on the faculty of the Franklin Pierce Law Center.

RICHARD J. GERING, Ph.D. is a manager in Pricewaterhouse-Coopers' U.S. Dispute Analysis and Investigations practice in the Philadelphia office. This book contains a comprehensive chapter about Lost Profits because of his efforts. His experience focuses on providing consulting and expert witness assistance to clients and counsel in commercial disputes, with emphasis on intellectual property, breach of contract, labor, and antitrust issues. He has testified as a damages expert many times and brings clarity to complex matters. He actively participates in the American Bar Association, American Economic Association, National Association of Forensic Economics, American Law and Economics Association, Philadelphia Council of Business Economists, and Licensing Executives Society.

Contents

CHAPTER 3   PROFIT CONTRIBUTION FROM INTELLECTUAL PROPERTY

CHAPTER 4   LOST-PROFIT CALCULATIONS

1

The Dominance of Intellectual Property

Intellectual property is the central resource for creating wealth in almost all industries. The foundation of commercial power has shifted from capital resources to intellectual property. In fact, the definition of capital resources is shifting. No longer does the term capital resource bring to mind balance sheets of cash or pictures of sprawling manufacturing plants. The definition of capital includes intellectual property such as technological know-how, patents, trademarks, copyrights, and trade secrets. Corporations once dominated industries by acquiring and managing extensive holdings of natural resources and manufacturing facilities. Barriers to entry were high because enormous amounts of fixed asset investments were required to displace well-entrenched players. Today, companies that once dominated industries are finding themselves fighting for survival. Up-start companies are creating new products and services based, not on extensive natural resource holdings or cash hordes, but on intellectual property resources. Management of these properties will determine the winners from the losers in the decades ahead.

1.1 ECLECTIC SCIENCE

Dr. Leroy Hood was recently featured in a front-page story of *The Wall Street Journal*. He is in the business of automating the process biotechnology scientists' follow to find the defective genes underlying cancer. The search must be conducted among the 100,000 genes that comprise the human species. Making matters more complicated, the current process is slow and tedious because precisely measured solutions must be manually shuttled among hundreds of test tubes. Dr. Hood is changing the process by combining a broad range of technologies.

One of his machines identifies the sequence of the three billion molecules that make up human DNA and does it 60 times faster than manual methods. He has accomplished this by bringing biotechnology together with computer science, mechanical engineering, physics, liquid science, optics, and electronics. Dr. Hood exemplifies the trend that all businesses must now follow if they are to be successful. He marries established ideas and technologies from far flung fields.

In less than ten years corporations have been faced with technological advances including the continued miniaturization of electronics and widespread communications without wires. Surgical equipment manufacturers are facing increased use of noninvasive surgical techniques. Computer makers have seen their mainframe businesses literally reduced to, and replaced by, a tabletop model. CD-ROMs are killing traditional encyclopedia sales. All of these changes are technology based. As a result, all corporations need more technology and it is often the kind they do not possess. The New World order is defined by change. The leaders in this tumultuous environment will be those that embrace change. Change is coming fast and it keeps coming—all driven by technology. Time to gain expertise in all the different technologies required to compete does not exist. There is no room for the old "not-invented-here" mindset. The pace of change does not afford any company the luxury of developing expertise in all the divergent technologies that it needs. It is even doubtful that such a wide ranging goal could be accomplished.

1.2 PARADIGM SHIFT

In the world before the Industrial Revolution, early man moved away from a hunter-gatherer economy to an agriculturally based economy. Our ancestors roamed across large expanses in search of animals to hunt. Self-sufficiency dominated this model. A major shift occurred when early humans decided to stay in one place and grow the materials that they needed for survival. As an enterprise, agriculture employed virtually everyone in the world not living in the cities and used them in a series of repetitive tasks, done sequentially every season; preparing the ground, seeding, tending, harvesting. Then the cycle was repeated. In the agricultural paradigm, the amount of sun, rain, and temperature were vital to a successful season. People became accustomed to dealing with cycles measured in terms of days and seasons. Most farms were small and capable of supporting only one family, reinforcing mankind's desire to be self-sufficient. Over time, however, it became clear to some that the agricultural society was constrained by two key elements: labor and land. Farming at a higher level of output—above mere subsistence—required more land and more labor. Expansion of the agricultural economy required collective work and abandoning elements of self-sufficiency.

The Industrial Revolution created a new paradigm. Fueled by a world-wide affluence and an expanding population, the industrial revolution was triggered by technology and the realization that some products could be mass-produced and sold much more cheaply than similar hand-crafted products. The new paradigm of economic behavior evolved into one requiring large amounts of capital for the purchase of buildings, machinery, and equipment. Companies were formed to raise the needed capital and individualism initially took another step backwards. The new companies soon learned that the cost of producing their goods meant not only controlling the manufacture of products, but also that vertical integration enhanced cost controls and profits. Soon, large companies were acquiring their suppliers of coal, suppliers of rail transportation, and finally the retailers that sold the manufactured products. The new mega-companies desired to become entirely independent with regard to all of the functions required to obtain raw materials, produce sub-assemblies and component parts, produce finished goods, and retail them to the consumer. Self-sufficiency once again reigned, but this time in the form of a different kind of collective: the mega-company.

The Intellectual Property Age is now upon us and the new paradigm is yet to be fully played out, but clearly the trend again continues away from independence and toward a vital need for the talents of others. Interdependence is at the root of the paradigm shift taking place. Technology management in the future will center on leveraging technology that is owned to gain access to technology that is needed. Sharing technology is a concept many will find difficult to accept but accept it they must. Denis Waitley writes in *Empires of the Mind,*[1] "The leaders of the present and the future will be champions of cooperation more often than of competition. While the power to maintain access to resources will remain important, 'the survival of the fittest' mentality will give away to survival of the wisest, a philosophy of understanding, cooperation, knowledge, and reason." Access to vital resources has changed because the nature of the most important resources is no longer embodied in fixed material assets. Gaining access to technology means cooperating with other companies, even competitors, in order to gain access to their knowledge-based resources. Independence is being replaced by interdependence. Waitley succinctly explains, "The future leaders will only get what they want by helping others get what they want." This point was previously illustrated by the story about Dr. Leroy Hood who uses technology from far-flung fields to accomplish his goals.

1.3 LOOKING AT INTELLECTUAL PROPERTY VALUE

Intangible assets and intellectual property dominate the value of businesses. Here is a comparison of the market value of selected companies with the accounting value presented on their respective balance sheets.

---

[1]Denis Waitley. *Empires of the Mind—Lessons to Lead and Succeed in a Knowledge-Based World,* New York: William Morrow and Company, Inc., 1995, page 8.

The market value has been determined by combining the total stock value of shareholders' equity and the book value of long-term debt.[2] When this value is compared to the balance sheet for different asset categories a huge gap of value is identified. The gap represents the aggregate value of all intangible assets and intellectual property of a company.

A diverse group of companies has been selected for this analysis. They represent a broad cross-section of industries, all of which show a significant gap in accounting for intellectual property and intangible asset values.[3] The following companies have been selected to demonstrate the dominance of intangible assets and intellectual property, not only for specific companies but also for a broad cross section of industries:

Company	Industry
Heinz	Food
Johnson & Johnson	Medical
Merck	Pharmaceutical
Microsoft	Computer Software
Minnesota, Mining & Manufacturing (3M)	Industrial
Philip Morris	Tobacco
Nike	Apparel
Procter & Gamble	Consumer

(a) H. J. Heinz Company

H. J. Heinz is not a glitzy entertainment company or a high-tech telecommunications company. Heinz is a food company that is the leading producer of ketchup with over 50 percent of the U.S. market.

---

[2] For this analysis we have assumed that the book value of the long-term debt of each company fairly represents the value at which these debt securities would trade as investments.

[3] For an additional presentation of similar data for a larger group of companies, see Gordon V. Smith, *Trademark Valuation,* New York: John Wiley & Sons, 1996, pp. 156–7.

Trademarks set this company apart from the pack. The Heinz name is placed on sauces, baby food, beans, vinegar, and pickles. A worldwide producer of food products, the company has a stable of well-known trademarks including Ore-Ida, 9-Lives, Chico-San, Orlando, Olivine, Plasion, Sperlari, Gulso, and Weight Watchers. Heinz enjoys the number one brand position in over 50 percent of its products.

Revenues at Heinz have steadily increased from $7 billion in 1994 to $9.3 billion in 1997. Operating profits for 1997 were 8 percent of revenues. As might be expected, Heinz had a significant investment in working capital and fixed assets. Inventories alone accounted for $1.4 billion of the total $8.4 billion in assets. The business enterprise value, on an accounting basis, totaled $5.6 billion.[4]

The value of invested capital for Heinz is calculated below. Equity is valued at the September 15, 1997 stock market price times the number of shares outstanding. The debt component is valued at the book value of long term debt. Together, the equity and debt values indicate that the value of the Heinz enterprise is over $20 billion.

H. J. Heinz	
Shares	369.3
Price	45.1
Value of Equity	16,664.7
Long-term Debt	3,425.1
Value of Invested Capital	**20,089.8**

---

[4] The business enterprise is defined as net working capital plus fixed assets plus intangible assets, where intangible assets include intellectual property. Other long-term assets not classified elsewhere are typically investments in uncontrolled subsidiaries and joint ventures. For Heinz the business enterprise value consists of fixed assets ($2.5 billion) plus intangible assets ($2.4 billion) plus other long-term assets ($0 billion) plus net working capital ($0.7 billion). The total is $5.6 billion.

Using the market value of invested capital and the book value of fixed assets, working capital, and other assets, a calculation for the value of intellectual property and intangible assets is represented by a residual. As shown below a more accurate accounting for intangible assets and intellectual property is a value of over $16 billion.

Heinz is a mature company in a stable industry with brand names that have existed for 100 years. Yet, the balance sheet does not adequately reflect the value of assets that are most vital to the Heinz business.

H. J. Heinz		
Value of Invested Capital	100.0%	20,089.8
Net Working Capital	3.5%	706.3
Fixed Assets	12.3%	2,479.2
Other Assets	2.6%	514.8
Intellectual Property & Intangible Assets	81.6%	*16,389.5*

Exhibit 1.1 shows the total amount of invested capital allocated among general assets categories of the company. For Heinz, 81.6 percent of the value of the enterprise is associated with intellectual property and intangible assets.

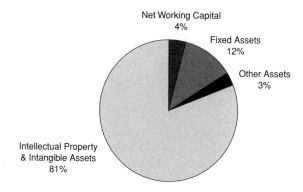

Exhibit 1.1   Heinz Allocation of Value

(b) Johnson & Johnson

The same analysis as just performed for Heinz shows that Johnson & Johnson has enormous amounts of intangible assets and intellectual property. In 1886 two brothers developed a dry sterilization process for the production of surgical dressings that were wrapped and sealed in separate packages and ready for immediate use. Innovative process technology and packaging are still the driving force behind J&J which has expanded into one of the broadest product line companies in the health care industry. Also propelling the success of J&J are its well-recognized trademarks. Product categories include consumer goods, ethical drugs, over-the-counter pharmaceutical, medical instrumentals, surgical supplies, and dental products. The company's Jansen Research group is well regarded for efficient commercialization of new discoveries. Jansen commercializes a new product for every 1000 compounds that it synthesizes which is four times the industry rate.

At the end of 1996 revenues exceeded $21.6 billion. Operating profits nearly reached 20 percent of revenues. The business enterprise value, on an accounting basis, totaled $14.5 billion.[5] On a market value basis the value of invested capital was over $80 billion and the intangible assets and intellectual property represented 86 percent of the company value.

(c) Merck & Company

Merck is one of the world's largest ethical drug manufacturers. Products are manufactured for both human and animal use. The emphasis

---

[5] The business enterprise is defined as net working capital plus fixed assets plus intangible assets, where intangible assets include intellectual property. Other long-term assets not classified elsewhere are typically investments in uncontrolled subsidiaries and joint ventures. For Johnson & Johnson, the business enterprise value consists of fixed assets ($5.6 billion) plus intangible assets ($3.1 billion) plus other long-term assets ($1.6 billion) plus net working capital ($4.2 billion). The total is $14.5 billion.

at Merck is on innovative research and patented drugs. Last year the company spent nearly $1.5 billion on R&D, an 18 percent increase over the previous year. From this investment comes patented drugs that command annual sales levels of $500 million and profit margins that can exceed 80 percent.

Strategic alliances provide a special opportunity for enhanced value with Merck. In addition to a joint venture with Johnson & Johnson, Merck has entered into a research and marketing collaboration with Du Pont. The focus is on the discovery of a class of novel therapeutic agents that promise to be the next generation of prescription medicines for treating high blood pressure and heart disease.

Scientific development is the foundation of Merck. Between December 1993 and 1996 revenues at Merck had almost doubled from $10.5 billion to $19.8 billion. Operating profits for 1996 nearly reached an extraordinary 30 percent. The balance sheet showed that the company had $2 billion in cash alone in 1996. Research facilities dominated the balance sheet where total fixed assets were shown to have had a net book value of $5.9 billion. The business enterprise value on an accounting basis was $16.9 billion.[6] On a market value basis, the invested capital of the company is valued at $70 billion with 81.9 percent of the value of the enterprise associated with intellectual property and intangible assets.

(d) Microsoft Corporation

Microsoft has developed a broad line of systems software and applications software for microcomputers. The systems software of the

---

[6] The business enterprise is defined as net working capital plus fixed assets plus intangible assets, where intangible assets include intellectual property. Other long-term assets not classified elsewhere are typically investments in uncontrolled subsidiaries and joint ventures. For Merck the business enterprise value consists of fixed assets ($5.9 billion) plus intangible assets ($6.7 billion) plus other long-term assets ($1.4 billion) plus net working capital ($2.9 billion). The total is $16.9 billion.

company began with the MS-DOS operating system, which was the most widely used system for IBM-compatible computers. From that base the company has expanded its product offerings beyond operating software. Applications software produced by the company include highly acclaimed spreadsheet programs, word processors, file managers, project managers, communications programs, graphic programs, data base management, games, internet browsers, and money management programs. The company also sells a large assortment of books that help customers get the most out of the company's programs. In addition, the company sells CD-ROM products, interface products, and other peripheral hardware. Microsoft has interests in every form of information collection and manipulation service or product that exists—all derived from a $10,000 investment in the basic code for its original disk operating system.

In 1993 revenues for Microsoft exceeded $3.7 billion. By 1996 revenues were $8.7 billion. Operating profits were 35.5 percent for 1996, which is better than the profit level achieved by the world's leading pharmaceutical company. Total assets of the company for the year ending June 1996 were $10 billion. Cash ($6.9 billion) represented almost 70 percent of that amount. Fixed assets totaled $1.3 billion with less than $1 billion shown as investment in other long-term assets. The business enterprise value, on an accounting basis, was $7.6 billion.[7] On a market value basis, the enterprise is valued at $159 billion with an enormous 95.2 percent of the value of the enterprise being intellectual property and intangible assets.

---

[7] The business enterprise is defined as net working capital plus fixed assets plus intangible assets, where intangible assets include intellectual property. Other long-term assets not classified elsewhere are typically investments in uncontrolled subsidiaries and joint ventures. For Microsoft the business enterprise value consists of fixed assets ($1.3 billion) plus intangible assets ($0 billion) plus other long-term assets ($0.9 billion) plus net working capital ($5.4 billion). The total is $7.6 billion.

(e) Minnesota Mining & Manufacturing Company (3M)

3M is a highly diversified company centered on innovative research and new product development. The success of this company is driven by a combination of technology, patents, and trademarks. The industrial sector of the company produces pressure sensitive tapes, coated abrasives, cleaning materials, roofing granules, and specialty chemicals. Information and imaging products include computer diskettes, data cartridges, videotape, printing plates, medical diagnostic products, overhead projectors, and transparency films. The life sciences sector of 3M markets medical, surgical, orthopedic, pharmaceutical, and dental products. Consumer products include Scotch tapes, Post-it notes, and other office supplies. 3M is more of an industrial company than any of the other companies already discussed.

Strong revenue growth and high profit margins are characteristics of 3M. Revenues have grown from $11 billion in 1993 to $14.2 billion by 1996. Operating profits for 1996 were 17.3 percent of revenues. Such revenue growth and profit margin levels are not from a commodity business. Significant intellectual property and intangible assets are evident. The business enterprise value, as of the December 31, 1996 financial report, equaled $8.9 billion.[8] On a market value basis, the enterprise is valued at $39 billion with 75.6 percent of the value of the enterprise being intellectual property and intangible assets.

(f) Philip Morris Company

Philip Morris is one of the world's largest consumer packaged goods companies. Products include cigarettes (Marlboro), beverages (Miller

---

[8] The business enterprise is defined as net working capital plus fixed assets plus intangible assets, where intangible assets include intellectual property. Other long-term assets not classified elsewhere are typically investments in uncontrolled subsidiaries and joint ventures. For 3M the business enterprise value consists of fixed assets ($4.8 billion) plus intangible assets ($0 billion) plus other long-term assets ($1.4 billion) plus net working capital ($2.7 billion). The total is $8.9 billion.

Beer), and the food products of General Foods and Kraft. The intangible assets of the company are represented by one of the greatest trademark portfolios in the world. Included are: Marlboro, Benson & Hedges, Merit, Virginia Slims, Maxwell House, Yuban, Sanka, Brim, Post, Jell-O, Log Cabin, Birds Eye, Kool-Aid, Oscar Mayer, Kraft, Velveeta, Miracle Whip, Sealtest, Miller High Life, Miller Lite, and Lowenbrau. In the mature markets of Philip Morris, intangible asset magic is being practiced with the introduction of new products that extend well-known trademarks. Jell-O has introduced ready-to-eat puddings and frozen pudding pops. Kool-Aid is being extended with a line of ready-to-drink single serving products. The company has extraordinary cash flow from cigarette operations and is continually seeking trademarked product acquisitions to expand its line of brands.

Philip Morris shows a balance sheet (December 31, 1996) business enterprise value of $41.8 billion.[9] Intangible assets are shown as $19 billion of this amount. On a market value basis, the enterprise is valued at $125.6 billion with 81.8 percent ($103 billion) of the value of the enterprise being the intellectual property and intangible assets that are shown on the books at $19 billion.

(g)   Nike, Inc.

Transformation of the lowly sneaker into $9.2 billion of athletic shoe sales is the hallmark of Nike. Almost anywhere in the world the Nike name and swoosh logo can be found on footwear, jogging shorts, tennis clothes, sweatshirts, ski wear, other athletic apparel, and accessory items such as athletic bags. The company has exploited its technologically

---

[9] The business enterprise is defined as net working capital plus fixed assets plus intangible assets, where intangible assets include intellectual property. Other long-term assets not classified elsewhere are typically investments in uncontrolled subsidiaries and joint ventures. For Philip Morris the business enterprise value consists of fixed assets ($11.7 billion) plus intangible assets ($19 billion) plus other long-term assets ($8.9 billion) plus net working capital ($2.2 billion). The total is $41.8 billion.

advanced footwear by expanding the customer awareness that different sports require specifically designed footwear. No longer do weekend sports warriors have one pair of sneakers. Closets are now filled with different shoes for different activities including basketball, running, fitness, cross training, racquetball, and most recently, golf. One of the company's most valuable assets is the Nike trademark, which is registered in over 70 countries.

On a market value basis, the Nike enterprise is valued at $16 billion and 81.7 percent of the value is the intellectual property and intangible assets.

(h) Procter & Gamble Company

Procter & Gamble is a leading manufacturer of household and personal care products based upon a combination of innovative product development and the promotion of illustrious trademarks. Some of the trademarks include Tide, Crest, Spic and Span, Citrus Hill, Oil of Olay, Pampers, Luvs, Vicks, and NyQuil.

On a market value basis, the P&G enterprise is valued at $106 billion with 84.2 percent of the value being intellectual property and intangible assets.

All of the companies just discussed have significant intellectual property and intangible assets that drive their success. Regardless of the industry, these assets enormously contribute to revenue growth, profits, and ultimately to the value of the companies. As we have seen from the foregoing analysis, the investments in working capital and fixed assets pale by comparison to the value that the market has placed on the intangibles.

1.4 INVESTMENT PERFORMANCE

The stocks featured in this chapter were first selected as being a small stock portfolio of companies that are primarily founded on intellectual property and intangible assets.[10] They appeared in the 1991 book *Investing in Intangible Assets: Finding and Profiting from Hidden Corporate Value*, by Russell L. Parr. The stock performance of these intangibles-based companies has been very good. In late 1990, the following stocks were identified as being solid intangible asset-oriented investments. Assuming that an investor had purchased the stocks in late 1990 and held them until the present (September 1997), the overall investment return would have been 25.2 percent. This return beat the performance of the overall market as demonstrated by looking at the return on the New Standard & Poors 500 Index.

Company	Stock Price 9/14/90	Stock Price 9/15/97	Return[1]	IP&IA[2] Value as % of Total
Heinz H J Co.	16½	43⅞	15.0	82%
Johnson & Johnson	13⅞	57¾	22.6	86%
Merck & Co Inc.	22½	93⅝	22.5	82%
Microsoft Corp.	6⅝	130⅝	53.0	95%
Minnesota Mng. & Mfg. Co.	30⅞	89¼	16.3	76%
Nike Inc.	8¾	53	29.4	82%
Philip Morris Cos. Inc.	11⅛	41⅛	20.4	82%
Procter & Gamble Co.	32¼	135⅜	22.7	84%
Total 10 Issues			**25.2**	
Standard & Poors	265⅛	919¾	19.4	

[1] Returns reflect dividends.
[2] IA&IP is an abbreviation for Intangible Assets and Intellectual Property.

The successful companies that have been discussed have established records, strong market positions, and proven products, all founded

---

[10] The original list included Loctite Corporation. Since the publication of the book Loctite was acquired. As such, its stock performance could not be calculated for the same period. The original list also included Disney, but its negative working capital position detracted from the points being illustrated in this chapter, so it was eliminated from this presentation.

on intellectual property and intangible assets. In general, higher amounts of intellectual property and intangible assets provided higher investment returns.

(a) Intellectual Property Infringement Damages

Considering the value and power of intellectual property, it is not surprising that infringement lawsuits are proliferating. Too much is at stake to ignore infringement of such valuable property. Also contributing to the growth in intellectual property infringement cases are:

1. The complexity and variety of technologies used in seemingly simple products.
2. The significant investment in research and development that is lost when imitators enter the market.
3. Huge advertising campaigns that establish and nurture trademarks which are compromised by imitators.
4. Its potential use as a deterrent to those contemplating entrance into a market.
5. The enormous awards that have resulted for some patentees.

Each type of intellectual property has its own closely aligned definition of damages. Lost profits of the infringed are usually at the top of the list. When lost profits cannot be proven, or aren't considered appropriate, damages are often measured by a reasonable royalty.

(b) Patent Infringement Damages

Title 35 Section 284 of the United States Code (1970) reads:

Damages

Upon finding for the claimant the court shall award the claimant damages adequate to compensate for the infringement, but in no event less than a reasonable royalty for the use of the invention by the infringer, together with interest and costs as fixed by the court.

(c)   Trademark Infringement Damages

Title 17 of the United States Code Section 1117 reads:

Recovery for violation of rights . . .

(a) When a violation of any right of the registrant of a mark registered in the Patent and Trademark Office shall have been established in any civil action arising under this chapter, the plaintiff shall be entitled . . . to recover (1) defendant's profits, (2) any damages sustained by the plaintiff, and (3) the cost of the action. . . . In assessing profits the plaintiff shall be required to prove defendant's sales only; defendant must prove all elements of cost or deduction claimed.

(d)   Copyright Infringement Damages

Title 17 of the United States Code Section 504 reads:

Remedies for infringement: Damages and profits

(a) In General—. . . an infringer of copyright is liable for either—(1) the copyright owner's actual damages and any additional profits of the infringer, as provided for by subsection (b); or (2) statutory damages, as provided by subsection (c).

(b) Actual Damages and Profits—The copyright owner is entitled to recover the actual damages suffered by him or her as a result of the infringement, and any profits of the infringer that are attributable to the infringement and are not taken into account in computing the actual damages. In establishing the infringer's profits, the copyright owner is required to present proof only of the infringer's gross

revenue, and the infringer is required to prove his or her deductible expenses and the elements of profit attributable to factors other than the copyrighted work.

(c) . . . the copyright owner may elect, at any time before final judgment is rendered, to recover, instead of actual damages and profits, an award of statutory damages for all infringement . . . in a sum of not less than $250 or more than $10,000 as the court considers just.

1.5   OVERVIEW OF THIS BOOK

This chapter has provided an illustration of the importance and value of intellectual property. It then provided the basis for damages when intellectual property is infringed. The remainder of this book represents a primer that shows the basics for calculating infringement damages.

In Chapter 2, Business Enterprise Framework, the different types of assets used in a business are described. Intellectual property alone cannot be exploited without using complementary monetary, fixed, and intangible assets and this chapter establishes a framework by which to consider the value of intellectual property.

In Chapter 3, Profit Contribution from Intellectual Property, the means by which intellectual profit contributes to the economic benefits of a corporation are discussed.

In Chapter 4, Lost Profits, Dr. Richard Gering of PriceWaterhouseCoopers, presents a thorough discussion of how to go about calculating lost profits.

In Chapter 5, Royalty Rates and the Georgia-Pacific Factors, the 15 factors outlined in this famous case are listed and discussed as they pertain to deriving a reasonable royalty.

Chapter 6, The Analytical Approach, describes another royalty rate model that was expressed in a court opinion. An example of how it typically is implemented is provided.

In Chapter 7, Investment Returns and Royalty Rates, a method for allocating the total earnings of a company among the assets of the business enterprise shows a unique and comprehensive method for determining royalty rates.

In Chapter 8, Discounted Cash Flow Analysis, another financial-oriented model is presented as a means for determining a royalty rate.

In Chapter 9, Market-Derived Royalty Rates, the use of third-party licenses for determining a royalty rate that can be used in calculating infringement damages is discussed.

In Chapter 10, Royalty Rate Rules of Thumb, general methods that have been historically used to derive royalty rates are presented. Their strengths and weaknesses are discussed.

In Chapter 11, Trademark Infringement, Gordon V. Smith, President of AUS Consultants, brings order and logical discussion to the challenge of calculating trademark infringement damages.

In Chapter 12, Information Checklist, a general list of discovery information is provided along with the reasons that the information is important.

In Chapter 13, Settlement, the expenses of infringement litigation are discussed as going far beyond the costs of hiring lawyers, consultants, and experts.

In Chapter 14, Emerging Trends in Patent Infringement Damages Awards, Julie L. Davis and Kathleen M. Kedrowski, of Arthur Andersen, provide an analysis of 15 years of patent cases' damages awards.

In Appendix A, Theory of Investment Rate of Return, background information about discount rates and the weighted average cost of capital are presented. This information is useful for those that want to better understand the financial models discussed in the main text.

In Appendix B, Company Audit Reports Don't Show Intellectual Property, the inability of audited financial reports to properly show the value of intellectual property is discussed.

2

Business Enterprise Framework

Converting intellectual property into revenues, profits, and value requires a framework of integrated complementary business assets. Complementary assets are required to convert intellectual property into a product. These assets are needed to produce the product, package it, sell the product, distribute it, collect payments, and implement the many other business functions that are required for running a business. Companies that create intellectual property and then license it to others are still not free of the fundamental need for complementary assets. While the creators of intellectual property that license it to others may not need to acquire and use complementary assets, successful commercialization of the licensed intellectual property is still dependent on organizing such assets. Royalty payments to the creator are still dependent on the licensee organizing the needed complementary assets for exploitation of the licensed property.

Exhibit 2.1 shows the composition of a typical business enterprise as comprised of working capital, fixed assets, intangible assets, and intellectual property. It represents the collection of asset categories that all companies use to participate in an industry and generate profits.

Fixed assets include: manufacturing facilities, warehouses, office equipment, office furnishings, delivery vehicles, research equipment, and other tangible equipment. This asset category is sometimes referred to as hard assets. The amount of funds invested in this category can vary greatly for different companies, depending on their industry. As an example, huge investments in manufacturing assets are needed by companies participating in the automotive, aerospace, paper, semiconductor, and telecommunications industries. In other industries the manufacturing asset requirement is lower. Arguably, assemblers of electronic consumer goods fall into this category. Also in this category

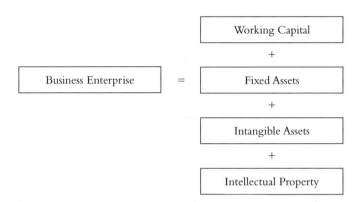

Exhibit 2.1   Composition of a Business Enterprise

are insurance brokers, computer software publishers, manufacturers of cosmetics, and many business service companies.

Working capital is the net difference between the current assets and current liabilities of a company.[1] Current assets are primarily composed of cash, accounts receivable, and inventory. Current liabilities include accounts payable, accrued salary, and other obligations due for payment within twelve months. The net difference between current assets and current liabilities is the amount of working capital used in the business. The investment requirements in working capital also vary by industry. The banking and insurance industries must maintain large amounts of working capital but in the hotel industry, where raw materials and parts inventory are almost non-existent, working capital is a minor component of the business enterprise.

---

[1]Current assets are defined by generally accepted accounting principles as assets which are expected to be converted into cash within twelve months of the date of the balance sheet on which they appear. Current liabilities are financial obligations that are expected to be satisfied within twelve months of the same date.

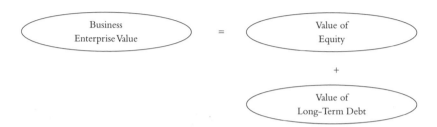

Exhibit 2.2   Value of a Business Enterprise

Intangible assets and intellectual property are the *soft* assets of a company. Generally, intellectual properties are those created by the law, such as the provision in the U.S. Constitution that established the patent system. Trademarks, patents, copyrights, and trade secrets are examples. Intangible assets are of a similar nature. They often do not possess a physical embodiment but are nonetheless still valuable to the success of a business. Customer lists, distribution networks, regulatory compliance know-how, clinical trial know-how, and good manufacturing practices are examples of intangible assets.

All of the assets of the business enterprise framework contribute to the revenue and profit generating capability of the business. They are also the underlying basis for the value of the business as depicted in Exhibit 2.2. The equity and long-term debt values represent the basis by which all other assets of a company were acquired, whether by purchase or internal creation.

Exhibit 2.2 also shows that the value of the same enterprise, as depicted in Exhibit 2.1, equals the value of the aggregate asset categories. The value of the enterprise is equal to the value of the equity of the stock of the company and the long-term debt of the company. These two components are also referred to as the invested capital of the company.

Exhibit 2.3 shows a more detailed presentation of the components of the typical business enterprise.

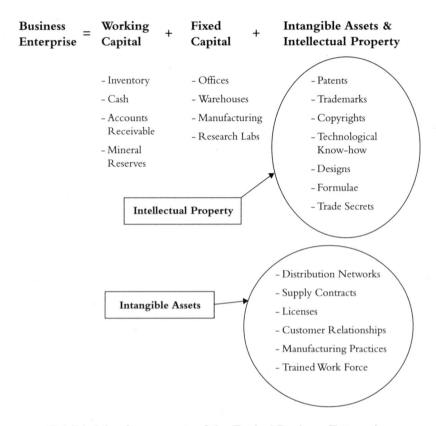

Exhibit 2.3   Components of the Typical Business Enterprise

2.1   COMPLEMENTARY INTANGIBLE ASSETS & INTELLECTUAL PROPERTY

After cash is invested and the machines are installed the facility is filled with bright light and hope as the electricians turn on the power. Light bounces off the proud industrial manufacturing monsters and employees rush from the parking lot into the building. The facility is poised for greatness, ready to . . . What? Until intangible assets are present nothing else can happen. Missing are the production procedures, assembly drawings, sales procedures, and distribution methods. Some of the missing intangible assets are mundane operating procedures that control the flow of materials and keep track of operations. Some of the missing intangibles are represented by the trained and assembled workers. Other intangibles are powerful computer software that uniquely control the workflow of a multinational company. All are important intangible asset components of the integrated business enterprise.

2.2 INTANGIBLE ASSETS

Intellectual property can be the most valuable asset owned by an individual or company. It can command premium selling prices, capture customer loyalty, and dominate markets. It can't however, manufacture itself, sell itself, or deliver itself. Intangible assets are a part of an integrated business enterprise that should usually be considered when isolating the economic contribution intellectual property. Some of the most common intangible assets are described below.

(a) Customer Relationships

Every business has customers, but not every business has customer relationships in the sense that they represent an intangible asset. In order for there to be a customer relationship in the sense of a valuable asset, there is some obligation or advantage on the part of either the business or customer to continue the relationship. These factors create some "inertia" which tends to maintain the relationship, even when there is no contractual agreement between the parties. Loyal contingents of customers that patronize a company regularly represent a continuing base of business and relatively stable earnings.

Some examples of valuable customer relationships include:

- Banking customers that maintain deposits at a financial institution. The stable base of deposits represents the lifeblood of a bank's source of funds. They also represent a convenient database of targets to sell new services.
- Subscribers to magazines, newspapers, and other periodicals. The demographics of the subscribers to *The Wall Street Journal* are the foundation upon which the paper sets its rather sizable advertising rates. Without the subscriber base, ad rates for *The Wall Street Journal* could not be maintained.
- Customers of an original equipment manufacturer for after-market accessories and spare parts. In fact, some defense contractors produce original equipment in the form of tanks, fighter jets, and artillery at a break-even amount knowing that an annuity of spare parts will run for the life of the equipment.
- Insurance policy holders for fire, casualty, health, and life. Insurance companies make a significant amount of their profits from investment of the annual premiums that they collect. The funds can be reliably anticipated.

A stable of loyal customers with an incentive to stay with the company is a very valuable intangible asset. Change-over costs for many customers might be so great that a disaster is needed to motivate the customer to switch loyalties.

(b) Distribution Networks

A business that depends on others to distribute and/or sell its products may also have relationships of considerable value. There are companies that sell cosmetics, cookware, and cleaning products in the residential market through representatives. These companies have no retail stores and the relationship with their representatives is extremely important. Other businesses may sell complex products in a highly technical market through "manufacturers representatives." While there may be a contract between the company and its representatives, it is usually one that can be terminated on short notice, and therefore does not ensure a continuation of the relationship in itself. Locating, hiring, training, and maintaining such representation can be a very costly process and, once accomplished, the relationship is an asset of value.

It is important to note that, in this situation, the relationship between representative and customer may be stronger than the relationship between company and customer. Therefore the company-representative relationship may be very crucial to the welfare of the business.

(c) Supply Contracts

Contracts can provide a company with a guarantee of raw materials. The guarantee may be for the price at which the materials will be delivered. The contract may only provide for an amount of raw materials that are guaranteed to be available. Such contracts provide companies with a reduction to their operating risks. Risks of raw material shortages or price volatility are reduced depending on the type of supply contract that the company possesses.

(d) Manufacturing Practices

These procedures usually take the form of documents. These documents are basically the directions about operating the manufacturing facility to produce products and/or services at a fast rate while assuring quality. Almost every aspect of a business will have some sort of instructions that pertain to accomplishing its function. Many are not extraordinarily complicated. Some however, are crucial to manufacturing operations.

(e)   Trained Work Force

Finding and training employees is an expensive proposition for most companies. Value exists for a company that already has in place an experienced group of workers.

(f)   Licenses

Possession of various licenses can be crucial to operations. Some of these licenses may be regulatory approvals. Others might convey rights to use the intellectual property of others.

(g)   Franchise

This term can lead to confusion. The term franchise is bandied about and too quickly accepted as the source of superior company performance. One security analyst defines franchise as "the brand name and all that it stands for." Like using the term etc. at the end of a list, the author of this definition just doesn't understand the many categories of intangible assets and intellectual property that comprise a company.

Traditionally the term franchise is used in the context of owning one or more exclusive locations of McDonalds, Jiffy Lube, Mail Plus, Sir Speedy, or Midas Muffler. A specific geographic territory is conveyed in a legal agreement where the franchisee may operate the business. High profits have come to be associated with many of these ventures and the term franchise has taken on some of the connotations of the term monopoly. Transference of the term to companies with well regarded trademarks and exclusive cache has unfortunately occurred. In reality, the assets that are truly involved with generating the superior profits, if indeed they actually exist, include trademarks, technology, distribution networks, shelf space, advertising programs, customer perceptions, and other valuable intangible assets.

(h) Goodwill

Goodwill is another term that has been distorted over time. Goodwill is typically referred to as an intangible asset but does not really represent an independent intangible asset at all. Goodwill might be described as the integrated benefit derived from the existence of intangible assets. "The idea of goodwill appears to have existed long before the advent of modern business concepts. P. D. Leake mentions some early references to goodwill, including one in the year 1571 in England, 'I gyve to John Stephen . . . my whole interest and good will of my Quarrell (i.e., quarry).'"[2]

The term goodwill eventually became broader (too broad), "In the simpler business organizations of [an] earlier period, goodwill was often of a rather personal nature, attaching in large measure to the particular personality, friendliness, and skill of the proprietor or partners of a business. . . . As the industrial system developed and business increased in complexity, the various advantages which a business possessed and which contributed to its profitability became less personal in nature. The individual advantages which a company enjoyed became more varied, were integrated with all facets and activities of a business, and thus became less distinguishable. Manufacturing processes, financial connections, and technological advantages all assumed increasing importance. Goodwill came to be regarded as everything that might contribute to the advantage which an established business possessed over a business to be started anew."[3]

The situation for major corporations is a little more commonplace. It is largely an aggregation of recognizable intangible assets and

---

[2] American Institute of Certified Public Accountants. "Accounting for Goodwill." Stamford, CT: *Accounting Research Study No. 10*, 1968, p. 8.
[3] Ibid., p. 10

intellectual property. Tearney finds that, "The term 'goodwill' is an old term that has outlived its usefulness."[4]

Many equate goodwill with patronage, or the proclivity of customers to return to a business and recommend it to others. This results from superior service, well regarded trademarks, product performance, advertising programs, or business policies that meet with favor in the marketplace. Individually these are discreet intangible assets or the attributes of valuable intellectual property. Goodwill is the result of possessing valuable intangible assets and intellectual property but it isn't an independent asset.

2.3   INTELLECTUAL PROPERTY

Intellectual properties are the spark plug assets that bring the sleepy monetary, fixed, and intangible asset investment engine to thunderous and profitable life. Intellectual properties are the most powerful assets a company can possess. They can command premium selling prices, dominate market share, capture customer loyalty, and represent formidable barriers to competitors. The term intellectual property usually refers to trade secrets, patents, trademarks, copyrights, proprietary technology, or technological know-how. It is property derived from the mind and protected by the law. A brief description of the primary types of intellectual property follows.

(a)   Proprietary Technology and Trade Secrets

A general definition of a trade secret can be found in the Model Uniform Trade Secrets Act:

---

[4]Michael G. Tearney. "Accounting for Goodwill: A Realistic Approach." *The Journal of Accountancy*, July, 1973, p. 43.

"Trade Secret means information, including a formula, pattern, compilation, program, device, method, technique or process that: (1) derives independent economic value, actual or potential, from not being generally known to, and not being readily ascertainable by proper means by, other persons who can obtain economic value from its disclosure or use, and (2) is the subject of efforts that are reasonable under the circumstances to maintain its secrecy."

Another definition is found in Section 757 (b) of the Restatement of Torts:

"A trade secret is any formula, pattern, device or compilation of information that is used in one's business, which gives its owner an opportunity to obtain an advantage over competitors who do not know or use it."

Sometimes trade secrets and proprietary technology inventions are not patented in order to avoid making them public. These are potentially the most valuable because they potentially can be exclusively used by the developer forever. They can also be most risky. If inadvertently divulged or independently developed by a competitor, the exclusive use of the secret is lost. Competitors can then enter the market with an equivalent product and start a price war, which is sure to erode profits.

(b) Patents

There are a number of reasons why the developer of proprietary technology may wish to obtain legal protection for the invention by obtaining a patent. The most compelling is when a large investment has been spent on research and development, the technology appears to have a strong market, and where there are competitors that are likely pursuing similar research. An important trade-off must be addressed in the patent decision. Keeping the discovery a trade secret allows perpetual enjoyment of the economic advantages for as long as the secret lasts. At any moment however, competitors can introduce the exact same technology to customers if they discover the secret. Competitive pricing will quickly erase the economic advantage. A specialty business that was based upon years of research and multi-million dollar experiments can quickly become a commodity business.

Seeking a patent requires disclosure of the invention. In return the inventor is granted exclusive use of a patented invention for 20 years after the date of filing, for patents filed after June 8, 1995. However, after the exclusive period the invention falls into the public domain for use by anyone.

Economic advantages are guaranteed only for the exclusive period. This allows time to recover and profit from the initial research expenditures. Without the exclusive period of exploitation it is unlikely that companies would invest in huge R&D programs only to have the new inventions immediately used by competitors. This is the typical situation in the pharmaceutical industry. In his book, *Patent and Trademark Tactics and Practice*, David A. Burge cites the case of Sir Alexander Fleming who discovered penicillin in 1929: "He decided against pursuing patent protection so that his discovery could be commercialized without hindrance, and be put into worldwide use as quickly as possible. The result of this fatal folly was that, without the shield of patent protection, no commercial manufacturers could be found who would make the investment needed to find a way to purify the drug and develop techniques needed for manufacture."[5] It was 14 years later, during World War II, that penicillin became available in commercial quantities.

---

[5]David A. Burge. *Patent and Trademark Tactics and Practice*, New York: John Wiley & Sons, 1984, p. 27.

(c) Patent Definition

A patent is the legal process whereby technology is turned into controllable property with defined rights associated with its ownership. A patent is a property right that is granted by the United States Government to the inventor by action of the Patent and Trademark Office. The right conferred by the patent grant is the right to exclude others from making, using, or selling the invention. Burge describes a patent as a "negative right." He explains as follows: "While the right of ownership in most personal property is a positive right, the right of ownership in a patent is a negative right. It is the negative right to exclude others from making, using, or selling the patented invention . . .".[6]

(d) Patent Categories

Utility Patent. USC 35, Section 101 which provides that "Whoever invents or discovers any new and useful process, machine, manufacture, or composition of matter, or any new and useful improvement thereof, may obtain a patent therefore . . .".[7] The word "process" typically refers to industrial or technical processes. "Manufacture" refers to articles which are manufactured, and "composition of matter" relates to mixtures of ingredients or to new chemical compositions. An example is the patented process invented by Procter & Gamble for making chewy cookies that have crunchy crusts.

Plant Patent. Patents are also issued for plants. "Whoever invents or discovers and asexually reproduces any distinct and new variety of plant, including cultivated sports, mutants, hybrids, and newly found seedlings, other than a tuber propagated plant or a plant found in an uncultivated state, may obtain a patent therefore . . .".[8]

---

[6] Ibid., p. 27
[7] 35 USC Section 101
[8] 35 USC 161

Design Patent. Design patents are described as follows: "Whoever invents any new, original, and ornamental design for an article of manufacture may obtain a patent therefore . . ."[9]. Design patents protect only the appearance of an object, not its structure or utilitarian features.

Animal Patent. The United States Supreme Court, in a 1980 decision, found that living matter which owes its unique existence to human intervention is patentable subject matter (Diamond v. Chakrabarty, 447 U.S. 303, 206 USPQ 195). This decision gave guidance to the Patent and Trademark Office Board of Patent Appeals in Ex Parte Allen, 2 USPQ2d 1425 in a similar finding. These decisions raised considerable controversy, but the patent process goes on:

"The U.S. Patent Office granted a patent for a genetically engineered mouse, ushering in an era in which private concerns can profit from and control such artificially developed animals . . ."[10].

Pending Patents. When a patent application has been received by the Patent and Trademark Office, the applicant may identify products containing the invention with the words, "Patent Pending," or "Patent Applied For." This action does not provide any protection against infringement, either intentional or unintentional, because until the patent is issued its validity is not known. It may, however, discourage copying since, if and when a patent is issued, protection will ensue from the date of application.

(e) Trademarks

Like all intellectual property, trademarks are created and developed by human effort and human reaction. It is becoming ever more costly

---

[9] 35 USC 171

[10] *Wall Street Journal*, "Patent for Genetically Altered Mouse Opens Era for Research, Spurs Protest," April 13, 1988.

to create and develop well-known trademarks. They have all the characteristics of becoming "collector's items," a form of art in short supply. In a somewhat less controversial mood, Ogilvy in 1983 said, "It has become prohibitively expensive to launch brands aimed at a dominant share-of-market. . . . The recent launch of a new cigarette cost $100,000,000. . . . There may never be another universal giant like Tide or Maxwell House."[11] These words have tremendous implications for companies that possess well-known trademarks. The giants that exist are rare and valuable. Companies that own these trademarks are in strong positions of economic advantage. The function of a trademark is to authenticate the origin of goods or services so that the buyer can select those seen in advertisements or previously purchased. Thus they can be thought of as a "guarantee" of a certain level of quality or performance. The most important economic advantage contributed by a trademark comes from the buyer's trust in the name. Customers are often willing to pay a substantial premium price for the characteristics of the product or the service that the name represents. A well-recognized trademark is, then, an asset that can be of considerable value to an enterprise.

(f) Trademark Definition

A trademark includes any word, name, symbol, or device or any combination thereof used to identify one's goods and distinguish them from those sold by others. An exclusive right to a trademark is obtained by continued use of it. Registration remains in force for a fixed period, which can be renewed indefinitely as long as the trademark is in use in commerce. Unlike a patented invention, a valuable trademark can be used forever. Included in this category of intellectual property are protection of colors, unique sounds, scents, and Internet domain names that are used by companies.

---

[11] David Ogilvy. *Ogilvy on Advertising*, New York: Vintage Books, 1983, p. 121.

(g) Copyrights

A copyright protects the expression of an idea, not the idea itself. Copyright protection commences from the time when that expression is fixed in some tangible form, even prior to its publication. Formal applications to governmental agencies are not required. In fact, full copyright protection is present whether or not the work is registered with the Copyright Office of the Library of Congress. A copyright owner may reprint, sell, or otherwise distribute the copyrighted work, prepare works that are derived from it, and assign, sell, or license it. If the author of a work created it as an adjunct to his or her employment, then a resulting copyright would be the property of the employer. Examples of copyrights include literary works; musical works, including any accompanying words; dramatic works, including any accompanying music; pantomimes and choreographic works; pictorial, graphic, and sculptural works; motion pictures and other audiovisual works; sound recordings.

2.4 SUMMARY

Intellectual property is fundamental to successful company performance but without the complementary monetary, fixed, and intangible assets, full exploitation of intellectual property is difficult to accomplish. This chapter has briefly discussed a business framework in which intellectual property is traditionally exploited.

3

Profit Contribution from Intellectual Property

Working capital, fixed assets, and intangible assets are arguably commodity assets that most businesses can possess and exploit. A company that possesses only these limited assets will enjoy only limited amounts of earnings because of the competitive nature of commodities. A company that generates superior earnings must have something special, usually in the form of intellectual properties such as patented technology, trademarks, or copyrights. The contribution of intellectual property to the earnings of commercial operations generally occurs in three primary ways:

1. Price premiums can be obtained from the sale of technology-based products where the marketplace is willing to pay a higher price than it otherwise would be expected to pay for products lacking the technologically-based enhancement of utility. When all or a portion of the premium survives manufacturing costs and operating expenses, the enhanced bottom-line profit margins are considered to be directly attributed to the existence of unique technology or other intellectual property.

2. Cost savings can enhance the bottom-line profits even when a premium price for a product is not supported in the market place. When a technology allows for a product or service to be produced and/or delivered at a reduced cost, the enhanced earnings are attributed to the technology used in the operations.

3. Expanded market share can also generate incrementally higher profit margins from economies of scale that come from high volume production. This can occur even when premium product pricing or manufacturing cost savings are not possible.

Gravel quarries are generally an excellent example of a commodity business. The product delivered by quarries lacks the enhanced utility introduced by technological intellectual property. These companies possess all of the typical business enterprise asset categories previously discussed except for intellectual property. They may even possess extensive amounts of intangible assets in the form of customer lists, corporate procedures, and favorable union contracts. Yet the nature of their product places gravel quarries in a very competitive position where excess earnings beyond those obtainable in a commodity business are not sustainable for the long term. Overall, profit margins in the quarry business are slim. The reason is the absence of intellectual property for which the company can charge premium prices.

Most valuable intellectual property provides an economic advantage in the form of enhanced profits. A premium selling price can provide enhanced profits or lower manufacturing costs can be the enhancement. Some of the specific ways in which intellectual property can enhance profits are listed below:

1. Command of premium selling prices.
2. Generation of sales from un-patented, accessory products.
3. Increased market share allowing for enhanced profits form economies of scale.
4. Enabling the use of low cost materials in place of more expensive raw materials.
5. Elimination of subassemblies.
6. Enabling the use of less material.
7. Reducing the amount of labor to manufacture, inspect, package, or account for a product.
8. Reducing shipping costs by creating a product that is lighter, smaller, or specially shaped.
9. Providing higher manufacturing speeds.
10. Reducing waste or rejects.
11. Improving quality output and reducing warranty expenses.
12. Reducing the fuel or electric power requirements.

13. Eliminating or reducing environmental hazards, or improving safety conditions.
14. Reduction in the amount of investment required for working capital and fixed assets.

Barriers to competition are also an important aspect of intellectual property. Competitors are often faced with formidable obstacles when it comes to trying to duplicate intellectual property. Development time and huge research costs may be barriers. The absence of important background skills may also be a barrier. Whatever the reason, intellectual properties can contribute great value when they represent a barrier to competition.

Exhibit 3.1 illustrates the enhanced earnings that can come from intellectual property.

The first bar shows the profits derived from commercialization of a commodity product. All of the business enterprise assets are brought to bear but intellectual property is lacking. The commodity company has working capital, fixed assets, and intangible assets. Such a product might generate a 4 percent profit margin after considering costs of goods sold and general operating expenses. The second bar shows the enhanced profits associated with a product that is protected by unique

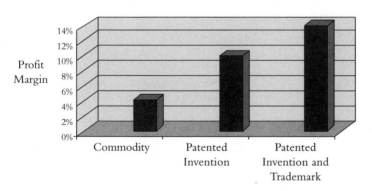

Exhibit 3.1   Intellectual Property and Profits

proprietary technology and shows that the profits in this circumstance more than double to 10 percent. When the benefits of a well-known trademark are added to the patented product, profits increase to a higher level of 14 percent (as shown in the third bar of this graph). It should be noted that the enhanced profit margins referenced above are hypothetical and used solely for illustration. The enhanced profits provided by patents and trademarks can be significantly higher or lower depending on a myriad of characteristics and factors.

Comparing the profit performance of two companies in the same industry can provide a further illustration. Both of the companies discussed below participate in the personal and household products industry. The primary difference between the two is that one has intellectual property and the other does not. The two companies that are compared are Block Drug Company and Bergen Brunswig Corporation. Both of the companies participate in the healthcare industry as described below.

Block Drug Company is a manufacturer and marketer of denture care products, oral health care products, consumer over-the-counter medicines, and professional dental products. For the fiscal year ended March 31, 1998, revenues for the company totaled $863 million and operating income reached over $57 million. The company manufactures products that are protected by patents and also markets products under well-known trademarks. Details of the financial performance of Block Drug are presented below as obtained from the Disclosure Inc. financial service.

Block Drug	Mar-1998	Mar-1997	Mar-1996	Mar-1995
Net Sales	863.1	862.5	715.2	621.1
Cost of Goods Sold	281.5	279.3	234.8	207.8
Gross Profit	581.6	583.1	480.5	413.4
Gross Profit Margin	*67%*	*68%*	*67%*	*67%*
Selling & Admin Expense	524.0	518.1	436.7	378.5
Operating Income	57.6	65.1	43.7	34.9
Operating Profit Margin	*6.7%*	*7.5%*	*6.1%*	*5.6%*

Bergen Brunswig Corporation and its subsidiaries are a diversified drug and health care distribution company supplying pharmaceuticals and medical-surgical supplies to the managed care and retail pharmacy markets. Sales for the fiscal year ended September 30, 1998 were $11 billion. Profits were not attained in 1997 or for the three previous years.

Bergen Brunswig	Sep-1997	Sep-1996	Sep-1995	Sep-1994
Net Sales	11660.5	9942.7	8447.6	7483.8
Cost of Goods Sold	11006.1	9368.9	7944.4	7036.3
Gross Profit	−654.44	−573.81	−503.21	−447.55
Gross Profit Margin	*−5.6%*	*−5.8%*	*−6.0%*	*−6.0%*
Selling & Admin Expenses	479.4	418.36	363.18	331.53
Operating Income	−1133.8	−992.2	−866.4	−779.1
Operating Profit Margin	*−9.7%*	*−10.0%*	*−10.3%*	*−10.4%*

Block Drug and Bergen Brunswig are both large companies with significant investment in working capital and fixed assets. Both companies have products to sell and customers that desire these products. They both have strategies, business plans, and active executive and middle management. Both companies operate in the same industry. Block Drug consistently makes a respectable profit while Bergen Brunswig has faced four years of losses.

The primary difference between the two companies, as shown below, is that the company that has intellectual property is showing continued profits. The company that lacks intellectual property shows continued losses.

Bergen Brunswig Corporation	Block Drug Company
Working Capital	Working Capital
Fixed Assets	Fixed Assets
Intangible Assets	Intangible Assets
	Intellectual Property
CONTINUED LOSSES	**CONTINUED PROFITS**

4

Lost-Profit Calculations

T he central question in lost-profit calculations was succinctly put by Justice Brennan, "Had the Infringer not infringed, what would Patent Holder . . . have made?" [Aro Manufacturing Co. v. Convertible Top Replacement Co., 377 US 476, 507, 141 USPQ 681, 694 (1964)]. The question may be answered by identifying and then quantifying the amount of sales that were lost due to infringement, and the amount of profits that the patent holder would have made on those lost sales. Lost-profit calculations are a function of sales volume, price, and costs.

The determination of the lost sales or volume, the price at which the patent holder would have made those lost sales, and the characterization of the costs necessary to make the lost sales are the central questions in the calculation of lost profits. This chapter discusses the framework and underlying analysis necessary for determining lost sales; issues surrounding pricing and the nature of costs including a detailed analysis of the difference in fixed and variable costs and the determination of incremental profitability. This chapter will also provide an overview of some of the major cases that comprise the analytical framework used to determine lost profits, particularly in patent infringement matters. Wherever possible, numerical examples are used throughout the chapter to clarify some of the theoretical points made in the text and to underscore the impact on the calculation of lost profits of various portions of the analysis. A list of some of the cases that have had a significant impact on lost-profit damage theory in the field of Intellectual Property is provided at the end of this chapter.

4.1 DEFINITION OF LOST-PROFIT DAMAGES

As previously noted in Chapter 1, the definitions of infringement damages differ slightly for patents, trademarks, and copyrights. Therefore, we must clarify those definitions to arrive at a definition of lost-profit damages.

4.2 PATENT INFRINGEMENT

Title 35, Section 284 of the United States Code (1970) states that: "Upon finding for the claimant the court shall award the claimant damages adequate to compensate for the infringement, but in no event less than a reasonable royalty for the use of the invention by the infringer, together with interest and costs as fixed by the court." The focus of damages in the form of lost profits in a patent infringement matter is the lost profits of the plaintiff (the patent holder) and not on the defendant (the infringer). In some cases, the profits of the infringer are considered as an indication of the profits that the patent holder would have earned had there been no infringement. It should be noted that the profits of the defendant are available as a measure of damages for the infringement of design patents.

Title 35, Section 289 of the code states that:

> Whoever during the term of a patent for a design, without license of the owner, (1) applies the patented design, or any colorable imitation thereof, to any article of manufacture for the purpose of sale, or (2) sells or exposes for sale any article of manufacture to which such design or colorable imitation has been applied shall be liable to the owner to the extent of his[1] total profit, but no less than $250, recoverable in any United States district court having jurisdiction of the parties.

---

[1] For the purposes of this chapter, "patent holder" is assumed to be male and may be referred to as "he" or "his."

Nothing in this section shall prevent, lessen, or impeach any other remedy which an owner of an infringed patent has under the provisions of this title, but he shall not twice recover the profit made from the infringement.

Lost-profit damages are based on an analysis of the additional amount of profits that the patent holder would have made but for the infringement. If the patent holder can show that absent the infringement, he would have made the sales made by the infringer, then he is entitled to the profits that he would have made on those additional sales.

> If in all reasonable profitability, the Patent Owner would have made the sales which the Infringer has made, what the Patent Owner in reasonable probability would have netted from the sales denied to him is the measure of his loss, and the Infringer is liable for that. [*Livesay Window Co. v. Livesay Industries, Inc.,* 251 F.2d 469, 471-72, 116 USPQ 167, 168-70 (5th Cir. 1958)]

4.3 TRADEMARK INFRINGEMENT

Title 17 of the United States Code, Section 1117 states that: "(a) the plaintiff shall be entitled to recover (1) defendant's profits, (2) any damages sustained by the plaintiff, and (3) the costs of the action . . . In assessing profits the plaintiff shall be required to prove the defendant's sales only; defendant must prove all elements of costs or deduction claimed."

Trademark infringement has traditionally been satisfied by injunction without monetary award. When monetary damages are awarded, the amount can be based on:

- Defendant's profits
- Plaintiff's damages
- Compensation for corrective advertising

- Punitive damages
- Attorney's fees
- Costs

Unlike patent damages, the plaintiff in a trademark action can receive the profits earned by the infringer for infringing activities. Plaintiffs in a patent case are limited to recovering only the profits that they failed to earn due to the infringement. In both cases the initial focus of damages is on profits.

4.4 COPYRIGHT INFRINGEMENT

Title 17 of the United States Code, Section 504 states that:

(a) In General—. . . an infringer of copyright is liable for either (1) the copyright owner's actual damages and any additional profits of the infringer, as provided for by sub-section (b); or (2) statutory damages, as provided by sub-section (c).

(b) Actual Damages and Profits—The copyright owner is entitled to recover the actual damage suffered by him or her as a result of the infringement, and any profits of the infringer that are attributable to the infringement, and are not taken into account in computing the actual damages. In establishing the infringer's profits, the copyright owner is required to present proof only of the infringer's gross revenue, and the infringer is required to prove his or her deductible expenses and the elements of profit attributable to factors other than the copyrighted work.

(c) . . . the copyright owner may elect, at any time before final judgment is rendered, to recover, instead of actual damages and profits, an award of statutory damages for all infringement . . . in the sum of not less than $250 or more than $10,000 as the court considers just.

Unlike in patent damages, but similar to trademark damages, the plaintiff in a copyright action can receive the profits earned by the defendant from his infringing activities. In addition, where the infringer's profits are less than the amount the plaintiff would have earned, then an additional amount can be awarded to the plaintiff. Plaintiffs in a patent case are limited to recovering only the profits that they would have earned absent the infringement. The same fundamental analyses discussed in this chapter can serve as the basis for quantifying patent, trademark, and copyright lost profits.

4.5 LOST PROFITS

Damages can be due to a combination of lost unit sales, lower units sales prices, higher costs such as increased marketing costs, and/or lost sales on ancillary products that are typically sold with the patented product. Damages from lowered units sales are typically caused by the competition due to the infringer providing customers with an alternative source of the patented product. The lost-profit calculation is based on the profits that the patent holder would have made from the sale of the units, but for the infringement, even if some of the components of the units were not patented. The patent holder can recover lost profits on the sale of products that include more than the patented feature. For example, the patent holder can include the sale of a kit in the damage calculation where only one of the components is patented. Lost profits are calculated on the selling price of the entire unit as adopted by the entire market value rule, as stated below:

> The entire market value rule allows for the recovery of damages based on the value of an entire apparatus containing several features, even though only one feature is patented [*Lessona Corp. v. United States* 599 F.2d 958, 974, 202 USPQ 414, 439 (Ct. C. 1981)].

It should be noted that defining the lost unit might have a significant impact on the amount of damages. For example, if the alleged infringed unit is part of a set of products, determining damages on the individual unit instead of the entire set of products will cause a significant change in the lost-profit calculation. Typically, it will be in the patent holder's interest to have as broad a definition of the lost unit while it will be in the infringer's interest to limit the definition of a lost unit since that will reduce the lost profits per unit.

Lost profits can be awarded for the lost sales of ancillary or accessory products. These ancillary products are referred to as "convoyed sales." Convoyed products are typically sold together with the patented product. In order for the patent holder to claim damages in the form of lost profits on the convoyed sales, the same "but for" condition must be met. The patent holder must demonstrate that, but for the infringement, the patent holder would have sold the convoyed products, and after subtracting the appropriate costs, made the calculated lost profits. The convoyed products may not directly use the intellectual property in question and in fact may, in certain circumstances, be the larger portion of the lost sales.

Additional and often specialized analysis is required in order to prove that a sale would have been convoyed. Consider an example of a lawn mower with a patented feature that was infringed. The patent holder is claiming not only lost sales of lawn mowers due to the infringement, but also lost sales of some grass catchers and trimmers. In order for the patent holder to demonstrate the positive relationship (both causal and quantitative) between lost sales of the lawn mowers and the grass catches and trimmers, the following types of analyses might be useful:

- Trend analysis might be conducted to help demonstrate a relationship between the patented and the ancillary products, that is, between lawn mowers, grass catchers and trimmers. The results of the trend analysis might show that for every 1,000 mowers that are sold, 400 grass catchers and 300 trimmers were also sold.

- Depending on the availability of data, the use of regression analysis might be an appropriate method.
- An understanding of the customer's buying decision is important in order to ensure that there is a causal link between the sales of the patented and the convoyed products. For example there might be a difference between first-time buyers and customers replacing an old or broken lawn mower.
- In addition, the product and marketing literature, coupled with an analysis of the incentives offered by the manufacturer to the sales force might be extremely useful in developing a causal argument.
- A detailed invoice or purchase order analysis of the patent holder's and the infringer's sales is often the most effective way to link the sales of the infringing and convoyed products. In this example, the invoice analysis might understate the lost convoyed sales since sales of grass catchers made on a different date after the customer determined that they wanted the accessory might not be captured in the analysis.

As an aside, it is interesting to note that the size and the profitability of the convoyed sales may have an impact on the size of the royalty that a potential licensee would be willing to pay to the patent holder. The interrelationship between the lost-profit calculation and the royalty calculation may be important in cases where the patent holder is claiming lost profits on a portion of the infringers sales and a royalty on the remainder.

Lost profits can also be the result of product price erosion brought about by the infringer's competition. Price erosion may be in the form of the patent holder being forced to decrease prices in the face of the competition due to the actions of the infringer. In addition, the patent holder can claim price erosion if he was not able to raise prices, or maintain his historic rate of increase in price levels, in the face of the competition caused by the actions of the infringer. The price erosion per unit is applied to the patent holder's lost sales and the *actual historical* sales made by the patent holder during the entire period for which price erosion is being claimed. Because price erosion is applied to both the actual and the lost sales of the patent holder, they may comprise the majority of the lost-profit damages claim.

The analysis of the sales price should look at the price of the patent holder's and the infringer's products before and after the time of infringement. This should be compared to the selling price of other similar products of the patent holder and other competitors, to show what noninfringing products sold at before and after the time of infringement. In addition, it is important to understand the marketing philosophy of the patent holder. For example, if the patent holder had a policy of not raising prices during a time period when competitors were steadily increasing prices, it may not be appropriate to claim price erosion during that time period. Lost profits should be calculated at the selling price that the patent holder would have charged had the infringement not occurred.

It is important to note that there are two components to the calculation: the price that the patent holder would have sold the product but for the infringement, and the number of units that the patent holder would have sold at the higher selling price. A correct determination of the elasticity of demand is necessary in order to calculate the number of units in the price erosion calculation.

This chapter will not explain the intricacies in calculating price erosion, particularly regarding the determination of the correct number of units that are to be included as part of the price erosion calculation. The discussion here is intended to be more general. There are a number of issues that need to be accounted for in the determination of price erosion in order to ensure that damages are not speculative or overstated. They include:

- The establishment of a causal link between the actions of the infringer and the price erosion of the patent holder's patented product.

- An analysis of other market factors including competitive products, noninfringing alternatives, substitutes, and the role, if any, of the infringer in developing the market for the patented product.
- In certain cases it might be appropriate to apportion the actual price erosion between the actions of the infringer (part of the damages claim) and other factors that are not related to the actions of the infringer and would therefore be excluded from the damages claim.
- It is a fundamental economic principle that people buy more of a product at a lower price and less of a product at a higher price, holding all else constant. The impact of this principle can be quantified by measuring the slope of the demand curve over the relevant range of quantities.
- It is important to understand the impact of the price decrease on the actual and potential quantity demanded of the infringed product, in order not to overstate damages.
- An econometric determination of the elasticity of demand might be appropriate in order to estimate the number of units that are subject to price erosion.
- In addition, as stated above, it is important to understand the role of the infringer and competitive products and companies. In economic parlance, price erosion is a measurement of damages based on a movement along the demand curve. Competitive products and companies may have been instrumental in shifting the demand curve outward. For example, the infringer may have decreased prices and employed a channel of distribution not used by the patent holder to create demand for the product with a type or class of customers that the patent holder never historically marketed or sold. An infringer that sold the infringing product at a much lower price directly to consumers where the patent holder only sold to the commercial market is such an example.
- It is important to analyze and separate the impact of the price erosion from other potential causal links such as a different channel

of distribution. If the patent holder would *not* have made the sale but for the infringement, then the patent holder is not entitled to lost profits and may only be entitled to a reasonable royalty.

- In certain instances there may be a case where the impact of the price erosion will be felt into the future, that is after the date of the injunction or the trial. It may be necessary to estimate how long it will take the patent holder to return to the pre-price erosion sales price.

A final note of caution regarding price erosion. The relative size of the price erosion component of damages has increased and the courts are typically requiring an increased level of sophistication in the economic analysis for demonstrating a causal link and actually quantifying price erosion damages.

Higher production costs can stem from infringement. At certain levels of sales volume, significant economies of scale can be enjoyed. Since the infringement results in lower sales volumes, the patent holder may be denied the benefit of some of these economies of scale, which may result in higher production costs.

Economies of scale that the patent holder may be denied might include:

- Discounts on the purchase of various inputs and raw materials
- Production efficiencies and cost savings due to the use of batch processes and longer production runs
- Longer production runs may also reduce manufacturing start-up and change-over costs
- Cost savings due to the ability of the patent holder to run two or three shifts and thereby lower the per unit costs by spreading their fixed costs over a larger volume.

Other costs that the patent holder might incur as a result of the infringement might include:

- Increased advertising costs needed to overcome the effects of the increased competition due to the infringement—increased advertising might also be necessary to overcome confusion by customers.
- The increased use of discounts, rebates, and warranties by the patent holder is another category of costs, although it is important not to double count these costs if there is also a price erosion claim.
- Increased sales costs and expenses due to the infringement such as the hiring of additional sales personnel and the diverting of managerial resources from other parts of the company to deal with the infringed product may also be appropriate depending on the particular fact pattern that is being analyzed.

Lost-profit calculations are based on defining the amount of profits that would have been earned on each additional sale, but for the infringement. These amounts are traditionally calculated on an incremental basis, as will be illustrated later in this chapter. The same analysis is also applicable to isolating the profits on trademark and copyright infringers.

4.6   THE PANDUIT TEST FOR CALCULATING LOST PROFIT

In order for a patent holder to receive damages in the form of lost profits, the patent holder must satisfy a test adopted by Chief Judge Markey of the Court of Appeals for the Federal Circuit ("CAFC") which requires the patent holder to prove that [*Panduit Corp. v. Stahlin Bros. Fibre Works, Inc.*, 575F2d 1152, 197 USPQ 726 (6th Cir. 1978)]:

1. Demand existed for the infringed product.
2. Acceptable noninfringing substitute products were not available to satisfy demand.

3. The patent owner possessed the manufacturing and marketing capability to exploit demand.

4. Lost profits can be quantified.

Exhibit 4.1 is a graphical depiction of the Panduit test. As can be seen in the diagram, if any of the four parts of the Panduit test are not met, the patent holder is not able to get damages in the form of lost profits and is only entitled to damages in the form of a reasonable royalty. The rest of this chapter will walk through the Panduit test and discuss how the test evolved as later case law has offered new interpretations and modifications.

Demonstrating that demand existed for an infringed product can be straightforward. If both the patent holder and the infringer have made sales of the product on a regular basis to informed customers, then demand is easy to show. Demand is often demonstrated by:

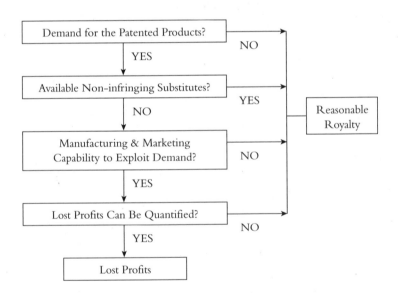

Exhibit 4.1   The Panduit Test for Lost Profits

- Showing the levels and growth of sales of the patented product
- Mapping the inverse relationship between the patent holder's and the infringer's sales, that is, demonstrating that the sales levels or growth in sales of the patent holder's products declined as the infringer's sales grew
- Reviewing the infringer's business plans and product literature which may speak to the importance of the patented product
- In the absence of good data, consumer surveys can be useful to show that customers would buy the patented product in question if it were available to them.

It is important to note that the demand for the patented *feature* is the essence of the first prong of the Panduit test. If the infringer is able to show that there is no demand for the patented feature, that consumers who purchased the infringing product were either unaware of the patented feature or that the patented feature was not part of their buying decision, then the patent holder may fail the first prong of the Panduit test and damages may be reduced to a reasonable royalty.

The second prong of the Panduit test is the absence of acceptable noninfringing alternatives. It is here that much of the analysis and interpretations of Panduit have occurred around the definition and proof of the three words "acceptable," "noninfringing," and "alternatives." The traditional interpretation of this part of Panduit has been that the patent holder must prove that there is a two-supplier market. A two-supplier market implies that a customer or a potential customer would either have purchased the patent holder's product or the infringing product. Therefore, absent the infringement, all customers would have purchased the patent holder's product.

The patent holder traditionally has a narrow interpretation of what a consumer finds to be an acceptable alternative. Under the traditional Panduit analysis, the patented advantages are used as an indicator of consumer behavior. The patent holder proves that there are no acceptable noninfringing substitutes by showing that the alternatives are inferior and that they do not have the distinct features and benefits of the product that has the patented feature. The infringer attempts to show that there are many acceptable alternatives and that it is not possible to demonstrate with any reasonable degree of certainty that the patent holder would have sold their product absent the infringement.

Often the analysis hinges on the interpretation of the relevant market and what the consumer was looking for when they purchased the infringing product in order to predict what they would have done in the absence of the infringement. A broad market may exist, but a subcategory of the market or a niche market might be proved to exist for the patented product in question. In the niche market, alternative products may be unavailable. Similarly, alleged alternatives can often be shown as having less utility. In other instances, alleged alternatives may have a significantly higher price so that they are not viewed by the consumer as an alternative. Alleged substitutes might be shown to have higher maintenance costs or not have all the features and benefits that the patented product has. The alleged alternatives may be less reliable or not available in the same size or product configuration as the patented product. An alternative product is not acceptable if it does not have the same benefits as the patented feature. The infringer has to provide an acceptable answer to the question, "If there are acceptable noninfringing alternatives, why did the infringer use the patent holder's intellectual property in order to make and sell their infringing product?"

In fact, the Federal Circuit has explained and clarified the meaning of an acceptable noninfringing substitute:

> "However, the mere existence of a competing device does not necessarily make the device an acceptable substitute. A product on the market which lacks the advantages of the patented product can hardly be termed a substitute acceptable to the customer who wants those advantages. Accordingly, if purchasers are motivated to purchase because of

particular features available only from the patented product, products without such features—even if otherwise competing in the market place—would not be acceptable noninfringing substitutes." (*Standard Havens Products, Inc. v. Gencor Industries, Inc.,* 953 F.2d 1360, 1373.)

An analysis of advertising, sales, and product literature and materials may be helpful in developing an analysis of acceptable noninfringing alternatives. Advertising materials are typically quick to promote new product features to attract customers. Indirectly, an analysis of advertising materials can show that customers purchased the infringing product because of the infringing features. Such an analysis also makes it difficult for an infringer to argue that customers did not know about the patented feature.

Often in the case of a dispute where one or both of the products are new, particularly in the consumer product sector, both companies had engaged in extensive market research. Market research and preference testing of products at or around the date of the product launch (that is conducted to test acceptance and understand what the drivers are in the sale of the product) can be extremely useful in developing an analysis of consumers' preferences and the utility of the patented feature of the products in dispute. These documents may be extremely useful in developing an analysis of acceptable noninfringing alternatives.

Even if an acceptable noninfringing substitute is proven to exist, the patent holder can still argue that it would have captured some of the sales of the infringer and therefore he is still entitled to some damages in the form of lost profits. An important question becomes, "What would the customers have done if the infringing product had not been on the market?" Some of the customers would have purchased the acceptable noninfringing substitutes. Some still may have purchased the patent holder's product. It is then necessary to quantify what share the patent holder would have obtained in the absence of the infringement. As explained later in this chapter, recent case law has dealt with this issue. In this case the market share of the patent holder and the infringer in the relevant product market are used to determine the infringing units that are part of the lost-profit calculation.

The third prong of Panduit is capacity. A showing of manufacturing and marketing capacity and capability requires the patent holder to prove that the infringed sales could have been made, and made within the relevant time period. The complexity of the analysis is fact specific. In an extreme situation, the determination of capacity may require a multi-disciplinary approach involving the damage expert with support from an engineer or someone with a marketing background in the specific industry. The analysis necessary to determine capacity may include a number of factors such as:

- The relative number of lost units compared to the historic sales of the patent holder. The larger the volume of lost sales claimed by the patent holder compared to his historic sales volume, the more difficult it may be to demonstrate capacity.
- The size and effectiveness of the sales and distribution network that the patent holder has in place compared with what he would need in order to make the lost sales volume.
- Channels of distribution of the actual historic sales may differ from those channels where the infringer made the infringing sales. The patent holder may need to demonstrate that he had the ability to make sales through these alternate channels of distribution in order to prove marketing capacity.
- It may be necessary for the patent holder to increase production capacity. The patent holder would need to demonstrate the ability (financial and technical) to increase production within the required time period. In addition, it may be necessary to adjust the calculation of the incremental profit margin to reflect the additional investment by the patent holder in increased capacity.
- In certain industry sectors, such as pharmaceuticals, increasing production capacity requires certification and approval from gov-

ernment agencies such as the Food and Drug Administration. These approvals may increase the cost or time required before the patent holder can increase production.

*   Analysis of the cost and availability of certain key raw materials may be necessary in order to demonstrate that the patent holder had the ability to manufacture the lost sales that are being claimed in the lost-profit calculation.

The fourth prong in the Panduit test is the actual calculation of lost profits, which is explained in more detail in Section 4.9. Lost profits do not have to be calculated with absolute precision.

In order to calculate damages based on events that never actually took place, the general standard of proof is one of "reasonable probability." Reasonable probability is somewhere in the middle of the spectrum of opinion; it is neither unfounded speculation nor absolute precision. Examples of how the courts have interpreted reasonable probability include:

"In proving his damages, the patent owner's burden of proof is not an absolute one, but rather a burden of reasonable probability" *Lam, Inc. v. Johns-Manville Corp.* 718 F.2d 1056, 1065, 219 USPQ 670 (Fed. Cir. 1983).

"In general, the determination of a damage award is not an exact science. The trial court must best approximate the amount to which the patent owner is entitled." *King Instrument Corp. v. Otari Corp.* 767 F.2d 853, 863, 226 USPQ 402 (Fed. Cir. 1985).

"The amount of lost profits awarded cannot be speculative but the amount need not be proven with unerring precision." *Bio-Rad Laboratories, Inc. v. Nicolet Instrument Corporation* 739 F.2d 604, 616, 222 USPQ 654 (Fed. Cir.) cert. Denied, 469 U.S. 1038 (1984).

In addition, it should be remembered that the courts have held that "when the amount of damages cannot be ascertained with precision, any doubts regarding the amount must be resolved against the infringer." (Lam Inc., 718 F.2d at 1065). In jury cases, "awards unless the product of passion and prejudice, are not easily overturned or modified on appeal." [*Weinar v. Rollform, Inc.,* 744 F. 2d 797, 808, 223 USPQ 369, 375 (Fed. Cir. 1984)]. As a practical matter, since the determination of what is "probable" and/or "reasonable" is subjective and difficult, the relative credibility of the damage experts is vital.

Damages in the form of lost profits may be expressed as an identity in equation form as either:

$$\text{Lost profits} = \text{Lost revenues} - \text{Incremental costs} \qquad \text{(Eq. 4.1)}$$

or

$$\text{Lost profits} = \text{Lost revenues} * \text{Incremental profit margin} \qquad \text{(Eq. 4.2)}$$

where:

Lost revenues are the lost units multiplied by the price per unit;

Incremental costs are those costs necessary to make and sell an additional unit; and

The incremental profit margin is defined as the profit left after the deduction of those costs necessary to make and sell an additional unit, expressed as a percentage of the unit price of the product.

It is possible to theoretically divide the lost profit identity into two parts: the "but for" lost sales or revenues, and the incremental profit margin. Section 4.7 provides a brief overview of some of the major decisions since Panduit that had an impact on the theory of damages through refinements in the interpretation of the determination of the "but for" condition. Section 3.8 focuses on the determination of the correct incremental profit margin.

4.7 CALCULATING LOST PROFIT AFTER PANDUIT

The "but-for" question articulated in *Aro* and the analytical criteria outlined in the four pronged *Panduit* test remain as the basic framework for the determination of damages in the form of lost profits in patent infringement matters. Case law and damage theory has evolved since Panduit with many commentators arguing that there has been a lowering of the threshold for claiming lost profits and a tilting of the standard in favor of the patent holder.

This section will provide a brief overview of some of the major cases and highlight their contribution to damage theory in patent infringement matters. Where possible, the cases and their contributions will be contrasted to Panduit without offering any commentary on the issue of whether the courts are changing the threshold or balance in favor of the patent holder.

(a) State Industries v. Mor-Flo Industries

In *State Industries Inc. v. Mor-Flo Industries Inc.*, 883 F.2d 1573 (Fed. Cir. 1989) the court modified the second prong of the Panduit test: Acceptable noninfringing substitute products were not available to satisfy demand. Before State Industries, the traditional approach was to require that there was a two-supplier market, in other words that there was an absence of noninfringing substitutes. As the Federal Circuit notes, State Industries was "the first time we have considered whether lost profits can be based on market share." (State Industries, 833F.2d at 1577).

After successfully proving infringement State Industries claimed lost profits on the lost sales that they asserted were attributable to the infringing activity of Mor-Flo. State Industries obtained lost profits on lost sales in proportion to their market share and a reasonable royalty on the balance of the infringing sales. While State Industries marks a dramatic change in the interpretation of the second prong of Panduit, the CAFC still retained the essential analytical framework of Panduit:

> A standard way of proving lost profits, first announced in *Panduit Corp. v. Stahlin Bros. Fibre Works*, is for the patent owner to prove: "(1) demand for the patented product, (2) absence of noninfringing substitutes, (3) his manufacturing and marketing capability to exploit the demand, and (4) the amount of lost profit he would have made." The district court relied heavily on this test and we have accepted it as a nonexclusive standard for determining lost profits. With only slight modification we think it fits here and confirms the district court's judgment (Id. at 1577).

State Industries holds that in a situation where there are two or more competitors in addition to the patent holder, the patent holder may be awarded lost profits on infringing sales for at least his market share. It appears that State Industries allows the patent holder to bypass the second prong of Panduit when the patent holder is able to establish his market share and focus the analysis on the other three prongs of the test. The court modifies Panduit by recognizing that market share is an important factor in the analysis of the "but for" question. It is possible for the patent holder to assert and recover lost profits in a market where there are other competitors besides the infringer.

The CAFC affirmed the application of the market share test articulated by the district court, but the test was only to be used as a substitute for one of the prongs of the Panduit test. The court therefore implied that the market share test was consistent with Panduit.

State Industries changes the analysis of the "acceptable" part of the noninfringing argument. Under the traditional Panduit approach, the analysis focuses on the patented feature; only products that have the same patent features and benefits are regarded as acceptable. The patent holder proves that noninfringing alternatives are not acceptable by virtue of the fact that they do not have the patented features and that the consumer would therefore not have purchased those products in a world where the infringing product was not available. The market share approach broadens the scope of the analysis to include the analysis of consumer behavior, competition, competitors, and the nature of the market. Determining acceptability is now typically more than an analysis of the patented feature. It should be noted that the patented feature is still a central issue in the determination of lost profits, as it is covered under the first prong of Panduit as part of the analysis of the demand for the patented product.

(b)   BIC Leisure Products v. Windsurfing International

In *BIC Leisure Products v. Windsurfing International Inc.,* 761 F. Supp. 1032, 19 USPQ 2d 1992 (S.D.N.Y. 1991) the court again refines the second prong of Panduit. In revisiting the second prong of Panduit, the court took the opportunity to go further down the road of economic analysis and recognized that Panduit 1, the demand for the patented product and Panduit 2, the absence of noninfringing substitutes, are related.

BIC Leisure Products, Inc. ("BIC") manufactured and sold sailboards and infringed on a sailboard technology patent held by Windsurfing International, Inc. ("Windsurfing"). There were at least 14 other competitors in the sailboard market during the three years of infringement and most of them used technology licensed from Windsurfing. Windsurfing had a market share of 29.2 percent, 25.6 percent, and 13.6 percent during the infringement period and claimed and was awarded by the district court lost profits in accordance with their market share in the "sailboard market" and its established royalty on its licensees' share of the "sailboard market."

At the trial BIC argued that there were in fact two different markets for sailboards: the relatively high priced "One-Design" boards sold by Windsurfing, and the lower priced entry market where BIC and Windsurfing's licensees sold their boards. BIC's argument was not that Windsurfing was not entitled to its market share under the second prong of Panduit. The BIC position was that since it and Windsurfing competed in different markets, Windsurfing did not pass the first prong of Panduit.

On appeal, the CAFC reversed the award of lost profits. It appears that the CAFC based their opinion on the facts that:

1. Windsurfing's sailboards typically sold for 65 to 80 percent more than BIC's.
2. "[D]emand for sailboards is relatively elastic" particularly at the entry level. Which means that consumers are very price sensitive at the entry level—a one percent increase in the price of entry-level boards will cause a decrease of more than one percent in the number of boards demanded.
3. "BIC's customers demonstrated a preference for sailboards priced around $350, rather than One-Design boards prices around $600."

The CAFC concluded that Windsurfing failed the "but for" test and stated that "without BIC in the market, BIC's customers would have likely sought boards of the same price range."

The court appears to reject the market share interpretation of the second prong of Panduit based on specific evidence as to the characteristics of the various sailboards. BIC had a lighter hull design that allowed for a faster more maneuverable board than Windsurfing's One-Design board. The fact that there were Windsurfing licensees in the market that were competing at prices similar to BIC's was an important factor in the court's decision. Because there was a substantial delay between the liability and damages phases of the trial, the court was able to benefit from a pre- and post-injunction "experiment." "Windsurfing's sales continued to decline after the district court enjoined BIC's infringement. . . . According to the record, the principal beneficiary of

BIC's exit appears to be O'Brien." O'Brien was a Windsurfing licensee whose price was between that of Windsurfing's and BIC's.

BIC does not invalidate the market share approach articulated in State Industries which modifies the second prong of Panduit. Windsurfing fails to get to the second prong of Panduit. The court rejects the lost-profit award of damages based on Windsurfing's market share because the court held that Windsurfing fails to prove that it was in the same market as BIC and therefore does not pass the "but for" test.

(c)   Rite-Hite Corporation v. Kelley Company, Inc.

In *Rite-Hite Corporation v. Kelley Company, Inc.,* 629 F. Supp. 1042, 231 USPQ 161 (E.D. Wis. 1986), 35 USPQ2d 1065 (Fed. Cir. 1995) the CAFC broadened the scope and interpretation of the "but for" rule that was traditionally used in Panduit.

Rite-Hite, the holder of US Patent 4,373,847 (the " '847 patent"), manufactured industrial equipment, including devices that secure vehicles to loading docks during loading and unloading. Two vehicle restraints made by Rite-Hite were at issue: a manual version (MDL-55) and an automatic version (ADL-100). The MDL-55 incorporated technology in the '847 patent; the ADL-100 was *not* covered by the '847 patent. In addition, Rite-Hite also manufactured a non-patented docking bridge called a leveler.

Kelley Company ("Kelley") manufactured and sold vehicle restraint systems in direct competition with Rite-Hite under the trade name "Truk Stop." While all three restraint systems were employed to accomplish essentially the same objective, Kelley's Truk Stop restraint system competed predominantly against Rite-Hite's ADL-100. The district court found Kelley's Truk Stop vehicle restraint to infringe the '847 patent and awarded lost profits to Rite-Hite on lost sales of MDL-55 restraints, ADL-100 restraints, and the non-patented levelers.

On appeal, Kelley contended that the patent statute does *not* provide for lost-profit damages on lost sales of items not covered by the patent-in-suit, i.e., the ADL-100. In addition, Kelly argued that there can be no damages on lost sales of the non-patented dock levelers, since the leveler sales were not tied to demand for the '847 invention.

The CAFC addressed two issues that had a major impact on the theory of lost-profit damages in patent infringement matters.

1. Are lost-profit damages recoverable on non-patented items if those items compete directly with the infringing product?
2. To what extent should the "entire market value rule" include non-patented items?

Lost profits on non-patented items. The test historically relied upon by the courts to determine lost-profit damages for patent infringement is the "but for" test. The CAFC noted that the Supreme Court has interpreted "damages adequate to compensate for the infringement" (in the words of 35 USC 284) to mean full compensation. It held that the balance between full compensation and the reasonable limits of liability encompassed by general principles of law could best be viewed in terms of reasonable, objective foreseeability. The court stated:

"If a particular injury was or should have been reasonably foreseeable by an infringing competitor in the relevant market, broadly defined, that injury is generally compensable absent a persuasive reason to the contrary" (op. at 1070).

Applied to this case, the CAFC agreed that but for the infringement of the '847 patent, Rite-Hite would have made additional sales of both the MDL-55 and the ADL-100 restraints. The CAFC affirmed the lower court's ruling, and included the ADL-100 restraints in the lost profit award:

"Here, the only substitute for the patented device was the ADL-100, another of the patentee's devices. Such a substitute was not an 'acceptable, non-infringing substitute' within the meaning of Panduit because, being patented by Rite-Hite, it was not available to customers except from Rite-Hite. . . . Rite-Hite therefore would not have lost the sales to a third party" (op. at 1071-72).

The court further stated that:

"[I]f, on the other hand, the ADL-100 had not been patented and was found to be an acceptable substitute, that would have been a different story, and Rite-Hite would have had to prove that its customers would not have obtained the ADL-100 from a third party in order to prove the second factor of Panduit" (op. at 1072).

The court emphasized that: ". . . Panduit is not the sine qua non for proving 'but for' causation. If there are other ways to show that the infringement in fact caused the patentee's lost profits, there is no reason why another test should not be acceptable" (op. at 1071).

Collateral sales. The second issue stemmed from the lower court's award of lost profits on Rite-Hite's non-patented levelers. Rite-Hite had claimed lost profits on these collateral sales based on the "entire market value rule," which asserts that damages may be recovered for an entire device or apparatus if it can be shown that the patented features were the basis for the demand for the entire apparatus.

In past decisions the court has ruled that individual components need not be physically connected, but must constitute a functional unit. Additionally, the court had discussed the unpatented items' financial and marketing dependence on the patented items. In this action, the CAFC clarified those past rulings, stating that:

. . . the facts of past cases clearly imply a limitation on damages, when recovery is sought on sales of unpatented components sold with patented components, to the effect that the unpatented components must function together with the patented component in some manner so as to produce a desired end product or result. All the components together must be analogous to components of a single assembly or be parts of a complete machine, or they must constitute a functional unit. Our precedent has not extended liability to include items that have essentially no functional relationship to the patented invention and that may have been sold with an infringing device only as a matter of convenience or business advantage (op. at 1073).

The court found that the concurrent sales of restraints and levelers were done for reasons related to marketing and construction scheduling. In the court's opinion, since the restraints and levelers did not function together, the entire market value rule did not extend to the levelers. As a result, lost profits on lost sales of levelers were not recoverable and the CAFC vacated the lower court's award of damages based on lost sales of levelers.

Implications. Rite-Hite has two major implications on damage theory. Lost-profit damages need not be confined to lost sales on patented products only. Rather, damages on non-patented items for which "but for" causation was shown, were recoverable. Rite-Hite is a broader articulation of the "but for" condition necessary for all lost-profit damages. The general rule for determining actual damages to a patentee that is itself a patentee that is itself producing the patented item is to determine "the sales and profits lost to the patentee because of infringement." (Rite-Hite, 56 F.3d at 1545). To recover lost profit damages, "the patentee must show a reasonable probability that "but for" the infringement, it would have made the sales that were made by the infringer." (Id).

The Rite-Hite case's second implication is that the standard for claiming convoyed sales has been clarified and appears to be more stringent. In order to claim damages on collateral or convoyed sales, the patentee must tie in the loss of the convoyed sales to the infringement of the patent. It is not enough merely to show that the collateral and patented sales were related in time or place; both function and causation were required.

4.8 INCREMENTAL PROFITS

The previous sections of this chapter, particularly sections 4.6 and 4.7, have focused on the theory of lost-profit damages. The theory deals with what the patent holder is entitled to—both as a matter of law and as a matter of economic principles—in order to answer Justice Brennan's question posed at the start of the chapter: Had the Infringer not infringed, what would the Patent Holder have made? Or, to paraphrase: But for the infringement by the defendant, how much more would the plaintiff have made? The remainder of the chapter focuses on the steps necessary to quantify the "how much more." It is important to remember that an inability by the patent holder to actually calculate the amount of lost profits may mean that the patent holder is unable to pass the fourth prong of Panduit and that damages may be reduced to a reasonable royalty.

Lost profits are a function of unit volume, selling price, and costs. Assume that the amount of lost sales has been identified, and the price that would have been charged is also easily identified because both the infringer and plaintiff charged approximately the same price, and there are no claims of price erosion. The lost-profit damages can be determined as the incremental profits that would have been earned on the lost sales. The method is referred to as the incremental income method [*Paper Converting Machine Co. v. Magna-Graphics Corp.*, 745 F.2d 11, 22 (Fed. Cir. 1984)]. The focal point of this analysis is to identify the costs and expenses that would have been incurred while making and selling the additional units. The costs that should be deducted from the lost sales are only those that vary with the changes in the sales volume at issue. Such costs are typically called incremental costs or variable costs. When variable costs are deducted from the lost-sales revenue, the amount of lost profits due to the infringement is derived. In fact, the calculation of damages in the form of lost profits, which is the subject of this entire chapter, should really be called the calculation of lost *incremental profits*.

The following equations are some basic identities that are useful in understanding the relationship between profits, revenues, and costs.

Profit is a function of revenue and cost such that:

$$\text{Profits} = \text{Revenues} - \text{Costs} \qquad \text{(Eq. 4.3)}$$

Where revenue is a function of unit price and unit quantity such that:

$$\text{Revenue} = \text{Price} \times \text{Quantity} \qquad \text{(Eq. 4.4)}$$

And costs may be divided into two categories so that:

$$\text{Costs} = \text{Fixed costs} + \text{Variable Costs} \qquad \text{(Eq. 4.5)}$$

Referring to equation 4.4, it is possible to define lost revenue as:

$$\text{Lost Revenue} = \text{Price} \times \text{Lost Quantity} \qquad \text{(Eq. 4.6)}$$

Combining equations 4.3, 4.4, and 4.5, it is possible to express profits in the following manner:

$$\text{Profits} = (\text{Price} \times \text{Quantity}) - (\text{Fixed costs} + \text{Variable costs})$$
$$\text{(Eq. 4.7)}$$

Since incremental profits are determined after the subtraction of variable costs, it is possible to define incremental profits as:

Incremental Profits = (Price × Quantity) – Variable costs   (Eq. 4.8)

It is possible to define lost incremental profits in equation 4.9 by combining equations 4.6 and 4.8 such that:

Lost Incremental Profits = (Price × Lost quantity) – Variable costs
(Eq. 4.9)

(a)   Definition of Variable Costs

Variable costs are those expenses of doing business that are directly related to sales volume. More sales means higher total variable costs. Variable costs are sometimes referred to as incremental costs since incremental profits are defined as revenues less variable costs. All costs are variable in the long run but the focal point for lost-profit calculations is the expenses and costs that vary for the volume of lost sales at issue over the relevant time period. If a certain cost category does not change with the increase in the sales volume calculated in the lost sales analysis of the lost-profit calculation, it may be regarded as a fixed cost for purposes of the analysis and should be excluded from the calculation.

(b)   Definition of Fixed Costs

Fixed costs do not change with changes in the sales volume. Regardless of sales volume, certain costs remain constant. Other costs are fixed over a defined range of sales volume and then change in a discreet manner. For example, rent may be fixed over a defined sales volume, but as the sales volume increases past a certain point, the company may need to expand, thereby increasing their rent costs.

Some costs are semi-fixed or semi-variable. Semi-variable cost is those cost categories that have two components. A semi-variable cost category will have one component that changes (increases/decreases) with changes in sales volume, and have another component that is fixed and does not vary with changes in sales volume. An example of a semi-variable cost is the cost of the company's sales force, where the sales force is paid both a base and a commission. As long as the number of salespeople does not vary, the cost of the sales force is a semi-variable. In this example, the base, or salary component of the sales force cost will not change with changes in the sales volume, while the commission component will vary directly with changes in the sales volume according to the commission formula that the company uses to pay their sales force.

Some costs may have what is referred to as a step function, that is fixed over a certain range of sales volume with discrete "steps" or "jumps" in the cost at certain sales volume levels. An example of a step function cost is a computer system at a company. Increases in sales volume over a certain range will not result in any changes in the cost of the computer system, so that over that range, the computer system will behave like a fixed cost. However, at a certain sales volume level, the computer system will not have sufficient capacity and the system will have to be upgraded or replaced. Since computer systems

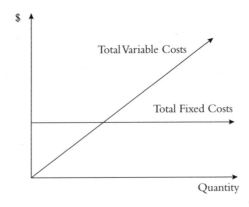

Exhibit 4.2   Total Variable and Total Fixed Costs

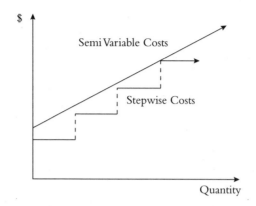

Exhibit 4.3   Semi Variable and Stepwise Costs

have discrete capacity and price characteristics, the cost of the computer system will increase in a step-wise function and then continue to behave like a fixed cost until the next system capacity constraint is reached.

Exhibit 4.2 shows the response of total fixed costs and total variable costs to increases in the sales volume. Exhibit 4.3 shows the response of a semi-variable cost and a step function cost to increases in sales volume

4.9   PROFIT AND LOSS STATEMENTS

A typical simplified profit and loss statement, also called an income statement, is shown below. The income statement summarizes a business unit's revenues, costs, and profits for a defined period of time. A business unit may be a company, a division within a company, or a particular product line sold within a division. A defined period of time for which there is an income statement might be a month, quarter, or an entire year. Often the internal accounting system of a company generates income statements that compare either the actual results for a time period versus the same time period for the previous year, or the actual results versus the expected or budgeted results. These internal financial statements, budgets, and forecasts are often very useful in assisting with the determination of which costs are fixed and which are variable.

The format is to list the revenues at the top of the income statement, and then subtract all the costs, typically divided into different categories, and show the profits for that particular business unit at the bottom of the page. A simplified Profit and Loss Statement is shown below.

Profit & Loss Statement	
Sales	$1,000,000
Manufacturing Costs	500,000
Gross Profits	500,000
Selling Expenses	100,000
Marketing Expenses	150,000
Research Expenses	50,000
Administration Expenses	50,000
General Overhead Expenses	50,000
Operating Profits	$ 100,000

Each category of the income statement is described in more detail below:

Sales.   Sales represent the revenue earned by the company during a particular time period. Sales or revenue may be further divided into gross sales or net sales. Net sales are gross sales less product returns, refunds, and other discounts that the company may have paid in order to have sold the products or services to their customers. Simply put, sales equals product units sold in a time period multiplied by the price at which the units were sold in the same time period.

Manufacturing costs. These are basically the costs associated with buying raw materials and transforming them into a finished product. This category is made up of amounts paid for the material inputs necessary for making the product, the manufacturing labor that is used to make those inputs, and the costs associated with the manufacturing. Manufacturing may include both fixed and variable costs. For example, it may include both the labor actually making the product and the cost of supervisors. The category may also include depreciation expenses for the manufacturing plant and equipment and property taxes due on the manufacturing assets. Manufacturing costs are the total amount associated with making the product or service that is reflected in the lost-profit analysis. This category of expenses in the income statement is often referred to as the *cost of sales* or the *cost of goods sold (COGS)*.

Gross profits equal to net sales less cost of goods sold. Gross profits are the amount that remain after manufacturing costs are subtracted and before any selling, general, or administrative costs are subtracted. The gross profit margin (gross profits expressed as a percentage of sales) provides an indication of the manufacturing efficiency. It does not, however, reflect the ultimate profit success of a product, service, or company. Many other important efforts required to get a product to market are not accounted for at the gross profit level.

Selling expenses. These expenses are paid to keep sales efforts on track. They can include sales commissions, sales staff base salaries, sales office expenses, travel funds, and all other costs of the direct efforts aimed at moving products or services from company inventories into consumer hands. Marketing expenses support advertising on television, radio, magazines, and newspapers. These expenses also reflect the costs to create, write, produce, direct, and record advertising messages. Packaging design is another expense that often finds its way into this expense category along with the costs of market research and consumer surveys. Research expenses reflect activities of the company aimed at developing new products and enhancing old ones. These expenses are not limited to those associated with new inventions. Continuous product development is often needed to keep pace with changing economic, environmental, competitive, and sociological forces.

General and administrative expenses.　These are mundane, but important, overhead costs for activities that support the core business of a company. They include expenses associated with income tax preparation and compliance, financial record keeping, insurance policies, human resource administration, management information services, control of accounts payable and receivable, and other logistical support activities. Depreciation expenses associated with fixed plant investments, other than manufacturing assets, are also often included in this category. Property taxes for non-manufacturing facilities are also included in general and administrative expenses.

Operating profits.　To arrive at operating profits, subtract all expenses, other than manufacturing costs, from gross profits. The result is the amount of profits generated from a business activity before income taxes are subtracted.

Depreciation.　This expense is calculated based on the remaining useful life of the equipment that is purchased for business purposes. It is a non-cash expense that allocates the original amount invested in fixed assets. Depreciation is calculated to account for the deterioration of fixed assets as they are used to produce, market, sell, deliver, and administer the process of generating sales. The depreciation allowance estimates the "using-up" of assets before calculating the amount of income taxes due.

It is important to note that there is no line item on an income statement that reads "Incremental Profits." Typically the incremental profit margin is lower than the gross profit margin and higher than the operating margin. In certain cases, often where the lost sales quantity is small relative to the actual historic sales levels of the patent holder, the incremental margin may be the same as the gross profit margin.

The calculation of the incremental profit margin requires a determination of which costs are fixed and which are variable over a known increase in sales volume. This determination is fact specific. For example, different lost sales scenarios in the patent holder's damage calculation may cause certain costs to be classified as fixed in one scenario and variable in another, which would require different incremental profit margins in the two scenarios. Section 4.10 below provides a general discussion of the nature of the costs in the income statement and should be viewed as a yardstick to compare the specific analysis that needs to be performed in each individual case.

4.10 FIXED AND VARIABLE COSTS

Each expense category of a profit and loss statement is a mixture of variable and fixed expenses.

(a) Manufacturing Costs

Raw materials and freight are directly related to the number of units being produced. More finished products mean more raw materials are needed for creating products. The freight charges associated with receiving raw materials would likewise reflect the added materials. Large order discounts might come into play if the number of infringed units is substantial. At certain volumes some raw materials can be obtained at discounts. If the number of infringed units is very large, the cost of raw materials, per unit, could be slightly lower than what is indicated by an initial analysis. In order for such a discount to make a significant difference to lost-profit calculations, a large volume of infringed units must be involved. Nonetheless, raw material costs are variable.

Subassembly components and freight are also directly related to manufacturing volumes. Manufacturers often have product components and subassemblies produced by others which are then integrated into final assembly. As with raw materials, the amounts spent are directly related to the volume of finished goods produced. Freight expenses associated with receiving these components also increase as more are delivered. Fixed expenses can be found in this category. The costs to design subassemblies and prepare specification sheets for outside manufacturers would not increase with higher volume, but these expenses are generally variable.

Manufacturing utility costs have fixed and variable components. Some of the power costs are basic for just keeping the lights on. Other costs are very sensitive to variable production. Whether one is using oil, gas, coal, or electricity furnaces must be heated and conveyors must run. More production takes more energy. Higher volumes require more manufacturing utility expenses.

Production labor wage and benefit expenses will ultimately vary with production. Increased volume may require another production shift which will require more workers. A slight increase in volume might be handled without more hiring, but it is likely overtime would be required. Overtime increases production salaries but not necessarily the amount of benefits. However, overtime hours usually involve premium pay scales. Regardless, more volume will cause higher expenses for production workers.

Supervisory labor wage and benefit expenses follow the pattern of production workers. If the ratio of production workers to supervisors is 10 to 1, then added production workers may require more supervisors and all the attendant costs. As small volume increases occur, this expense category can remain fixed but supervisory activities can only be stretched within narrow limits.

Quality control staff wages and benefit expenses may be controlled for slight volume increases but more production volume requires more testing. This must be accomplished by overtime or added shifts.

Hence, more volume will likely require more quality control wage expenses. One component that will remain fixed in this category is the amount associated with development and design of the quality control tests and standards. This expense should not fluctuate with added volume. For the most part, quality control staff activities increase with higher volume.

Quality control testing costs will follow the same variable cost pattern as quality control staff costs. Quality control often requires the use of testing materials that cannot be reused. Added production volume will require more testing which will require the purchase of more quality control testing materials. Quality control often requires destruction of a finished product to accomplish a test. A sample of each production run must be destroyed and this costs money. More production volume requires more units to be destroyed.

Licensed manufacturing intellectual property royalties can be variable where royalties are paid on production or sales volume. The licensed intellectual property may be separate from the property that is subject to the lawsuit in question, but nevertheless, it is still a production expense. A royalty on the sales of units produced will usually grow with added volume. If licensed technology is obtained at a fixed rate (an atypical situation) then added volume will not cause an increase in this expense. More likely however, is that higher volume will include higher royalty expenses. Care is needed in this calculation. Licenses sometimes include variable royalties which change with the attainment of milestones. At certain volume levels royalty rates can be increased or decreased. Most likely, added volume will cause licensed technology or trademark royalty expenses to increase.

Manufacturing asset property taxes are usually fixed. Added volume will not cause property taxes to increase.

The *manufacturing asset depreciation* expense is usually fixed. Depreciation is usually calculated by income tax formulas that do not have any association with production volume. Obviously production machinery will be used up more quickly by putting more product through the equipment, but depreciation expenses are not usually based on such considerations. Like a car, equipment has a finite life. More miles per year will wear out a car faster than less miles. The problem is that a very complicated study is required to establish per unit of production depreciation schedules and few companies conduct such analyses. If such a study is completed there isn't any assurance that the results would be that much different from the depreciation expense as determined by the income tax formula. From a practical point of view, depreciation expenses are fixed.

Environmental protection and scrap costs can vary with production. Increased manufacturing activity creates more waste and more scrap. Environmental protection for some processes requires the purchase of raw materials that are used to process waste. Waste removal of scrap is often based on a bulk or weight charge. More production means more waste, more environmental protection activities, more scrap, and higher expenses with added volume.

(b)   Research Expenses

Research and development is ongoing at many companies. New inventions lead to new products. New inventions also lead to new production materials and methods. The substantial expenses associated with research are many: highly compensated researchers; administrative staffs separate from the rest of the company; special research facilities; specialized equipment; prototype small-scale manufacturing plants; property taxes; and utility expenses associated with the research facility. Research activities also require the use of raw materials as new products and production techniques are analyzed. Huge amounts are spent on research but they rarely have a significant relationship to increased volume of existing products. The research activities associated with products in commercial production are mostly complete. Research activities are associated with future products and future production techniques. These activities are usually based on fixed budgets established by executive management. More production volume generally does not require greater research expenses.

(c)   Marketing Expenses

Product packaging design expenses do not vary with added sales. Once the package design has been completed additional expenses are not required. More volume requires the manufacture of more packages because each product must be packaged, but this cost is captured in the variable manufacturing expenses. The design work doesn't increase with added sales.

Advertising campaign development and production involves creating messages and designing commercials. Also in this category is the production of messages for different advertising mediums. Television commercials must be filmed and radio messages must be recorded. Newspaper ads must be designed and billboard pictures must be photographed. All of this is usually conducted in accordance with a set budget that generally does not vary with added sales.

Advertising placement for radio, television, newspaper, magazine, and billboards is another aspect of advertising that does not vary with added sales volume. The expenses indeed vary according to the frequency of advertisement appearances, but this has nothing to do with the volume of sales. A budget is usually established each year. It may be overrun but due to added volume. Event sponsorship is also usually based on a fixed budget. (However, golf tournament sponsorship might possibly increase when more sales are generated.)

Consumer surveys and market research are a continuing activity for most firms that sell consumer goods. Consumer tastes must be understood so that new products can be fashioned to address the desires of customers. This type of information is also used for improvement of existing products. Market research studies the activities of the competition and the strength of their products. Added sales volume does not normally cause more surveys and research to be conducted. These activities are usually conducted according to a fixed budget.

Display racking can vary with higher sales volume. If infringement caused the loss of distribution locations then the infringed party didn't have to spend the money required to provide the lost distributors and retail outlets with display racks. More sales could require more display racks for stores that carry the product and for stores that would have been customers if not for the infringement. At certain levels of increased sales volume, more display racks are required.

(d)   General Overhead Expenses

General overhead expenses are usually fixed costs involving primarily the salaries and benefits for personnel involved in management information, insurance management, human resources, accounting, taxation, purchasing, and engineering. These staff functions generally do not vary according to the amount of production and sales enjoyed by a company. However, engineering functions can sometimes be directly related to additional sales. Some companies sell big-ticket customized products to other companies. The sale of color printing presses to newspapers requires a significant amount engineering input. The presses must be specifically customized according to the location needs of the buyer. Conveyor and inserting systems associated with newspaper production also must be specially designed. Large ticket sales of customized equipment require detailed analysis from engineering personnel just to prepare bid documents. If the contract is awarded, then more engineering expenses are associated with customized production of the equipment and its installation. Depending on the industry and product, engineering can be a variable or fixed expense.

Another variable component of general expenses can come from the accounting department. Customer credit checks are often involved with big-ticket sales. Equipment manufacturers sell equipment on installment plans or offer financing from a finance division. In such cases the expenses associated with credit analysis increase with higher sales volume.

Executive personnel salary and benefit expenses can present an interesting dilemma. Some executives are paid bonuses based on overall corporate performance. While a few additional units of sales aren't going to make much difference, a large increase in sales could contribute to higher bonuses. Further complications are introduced by compensation programs that pay top executives big bonuses as company performance plunges, à la General Motors. (A penetrating investigation is needed for this category of expense.) Generally, a substantial amount of added sales volume must be involved before executive compensation becomes a variable expense.

Office asset property taxes are usually fixed just like manufacturing asset property taxes. Added volume will not cause office asset property taxes to increase.

The *office asset depreciation* expense is usually fixed. Depreciation is usually calculated by income tax formulas that do not have any association with production volume. Obviously increased use of office equipment will cause it to be used up more quickly but depreciation expenses are not generally based on such considerations. From a practical point of view, depreciation expenses on office assets are fixed.

(e)   Selling Expenses

Sales staff base salaries tend to be fixed but commission expenses directly reflect the volume of sales. Added sales will generate higher commission expenses. Some commission programs involve graduated schedules. As certain milestones are reached commission payouts increase. The first $500,000 of sales might not provide for any commission. A 5 percent commission on sales over $500,000 might then kick in, with a 7.5 percent payout on sales over $1,000,000. The amount of sales that can be handled by each salesperson is limited. At some point more sales people will be needed. A significant increase in sales will require more people to take orders, handle accounts, and visit and monitor retail displays. For the most part, a higher sales volume increases selling expenses.

Travel costs for sales staff can also vary with added sales volume. Selling big-ticket equipment to companies requires more visits to customer locations. Consumer product sales require more visits to retailers and distributors. The expenses might involve only added car miles but could also involve international travel involving airfare, hotels, meals, and travel sundries.

Shipping freight expenses increase as more product is shipped to more customers. Sometimes the freight expense is charged to the customer. Sometimes it is absorbed as a cost of making the sale. Either way, more sales volume will require more delivery expenses and these costs should be considered as variable expenses.

Promotions and discount coupons vary with sales. Consumer product companies offer deals: Buy one, get one free; Buy one, get the second at half price. These offers cost money. Each time a coupon is redeemed, money is spent. More sales can mean more coupons are redeemed and promotional expenses rise. Care is needed when analyzing this expense category. Sometimes these expenses can be planned to cap at a budgeted amount regardless of the amount of sales volume. When infringed units are added to the lost-profit equation, the promotional expense budget should be checked to assure that the budget cap is properly included in the calculations.

Table 4.1 summarizes the general character of expenses as either fixed or variable expenses. Although special circumstances will always exist, the table can serve as guidance for the deposition of cost accountants and other financial managers.

Each industry has its own character of expenses. Sometimes fixed expenses in one business can be variable for another. The character of expenses depends on the nature of the industry. Consumer products have one set of variable expenses and big-ticket equipment producers have another. A careful analysis and thorough deposition of

Table 4.1   General Character of Expenses

Expense Category	Reaction to Increased Volume
Manufacturing Costs:	
Raw materials and freight	Variable
Subassembly components and freight	Variable
Production utilities	Variable
Production labor wages and benefits	Variable
Quality control testing costs	Variable
Licensed manufacturing technology royalties	Variable
Environmental protection and scrap costs	Variable
Supervisory labor wages and benefits	Variable
Quality control staff wages and benefits	Variable
Manufacturing assets property taxes	Fixed
Manufacturing assets depreciation	Fixed
Research Expenses	Fixed
Marketing Expenses:	
Product packaging designs	Fixed
Advertising campaign development	Fixed
Advertising production	Fixed
Radio time	Fixed
Television time	Fixed
Newspaper space	Fixed
Magazine space	Fixed
Billboard space	Fixed
Event sponsorship	Fixed
Consumer surveys	Fixed
Market research	Fixed
Display racking	Variable
General Overhead Expenses:	
Executive personnel salaries and benefits	Fixed
Office assets property taxes	Fixed
Office assets depreciation	Fixed

continues

Table 4.1 *(Continued)*

Expense Category	Reaction to Increased Volume
Salaries and benefits for personnel in:	
Management information	Fixed
Insurance	Fixed
Human Resources	Fixed
Accounting	Fixed
Taxation	Fixed
Purchasing	Fixed
Engineering	Variable
Office utilities	Fixed
Customer credit analysis	Variable
Selling Expenses:	
Sales staff base salaries	Fixed
Sales staff or distributor commissions	Variable
Travel costs for sales staff	Variable
Shipping freight	Variable
Promotions and discount coupons	Variable

the infringer's personnel can properly identify variable and fixed expenses. The same analysis and questioning should also be conducted with personnel working for the plaintiff. Each expense category should be explored with an open mind. The urge to make assumptions about the character of expenses should be suppressed.

4.11 AN EXAMPLE OF INCREMENTAL PROFITS

Just a slight change in the allocation of fixed and variable costs can have a powerful effect on damages calculations. Exhibit 4.4 shows a calculation of operating profits for a company that sells 10,000 units of a product each year. Under the heading Base Case total revenues for the company are shown as $10 million; each of the 10,000 units sells for $1,000. Operating profit is the amount that remains after all expenses associated with making, selling, and delivering the units are subtracted from the total amount of revenues derived from the units. Each category of expense has been divided for this example into variable and fixed expenses. Some of the expense categories are dominated by variable expenses while other categories are dominated by fixed costs.

Research and development expenses in Exhibit 4.4 are all considered fixed, at the annual amount of $500,000. Additional units of sales are not expected to have an effect on R&D expenses. As discussed earlier, the research and development that is ongoing most likely has very little to do with the current products being manufactured and sold.

The fixed manufacturing expenses in Exhibit 4.4 are shown to be $1.5 million while each unit produced requires $350 of variable manufacturing costs.

Marketing expenses are shown to be heavily dominated by fixed costs of $1.75 million with variable costs of $25 for each unit produced.

General and administrative expenses are also dominated by fixed costs of $1,000,000. Variable costs per unit for this category are $20.

Selling costs are also shown to be dominated by fixed costs of $900,000. This would apparently indicate that sales personnel are compensated with substantial salaries and small amounts of incremental commission. In some industries, selling commissions are emphasized. The reverse is true and sales personnel are paid a small salary but receive substantial commissions for each unit sold.

Total fixed costs for all expense categories in Exhibit 4.4 are $5,560,000 and total variable costs associated with the production, sale, and delivery of 10,000 units are $4,250,000. Subtracting the total fixed and variable costs from the total revenues of $10,000,000 leaves $100,000 of operating profit.

INCREMENTAL PROFITS

		Base Case
Units		10,000
Sales price per unit		$1,000
Total Revenues		$10,000,000
Manufacturing Costs		
Variable per unit	$350	3,500,000
Fixed per unit		1,500,000
Total Manufacturing Costs		5,000,000
Research & Development Costs		
Variable per unit	$0	0
Fixed per unit		500,000
Total Research & Development Costs		500,000
Marketing Expenses		
Variable per unit	$25	250,000
Fixed per unit		1,750,000
Total Marketing Expenses		2,000,000
General and Administrative Expenses		
Variable per unit	$20	200,000
Fixed per unit		1,000,000
Total General and Admin. Expenses		1,200,000
Selling Costs		
Variable per unit	$30	300,000
Fixed per unit		900,000
Total Selling Costs		1,200,000

continues

Total Revenues	10,000,000
Total Variable Costs	4,250,000
Total Variable Costs per unit	425
Total Fixed Costs	5,650,000
Total Costs	9,900,000
Total Costs per unit	990
Operating Profit	100,000

Exhibit 4.4   Incremental Profits

Suppose that 2,500 units of sales could have been sold in addition to the 10,000 already noted in Exhibit 4.4. Suppose that infringement has been proven on a valid patent. Lost-profit damages are calculated in Exhibit 4.5. The fixed costs in each expense category have already been covered. The expenses that would be associated with producing, selling, and delivering the additional 2,500 units are only the total variable costs. Exhibit 4.5 shows the operating profits for the example company with the additional 2,500 units in comparison to the original calculation from Exhibit 4.4.

In Exhibit 4.5, fixed manufacturing costs are $1.5 million for both the Base Case and Added Units columns. The variable manufacturing costs are higher for the second column because additional units cost more to make. Variable manufacturing costs are $4,375,000 for the Added Units column. The amount is $1,375,000 higher than the Base Case variable manufacturing units, representing the $350 manufacturing cost per unit multiplied by the additional 2,500 units.

The total costs of research and development are the same for the Added Units column because no additional R&D costs are associated with the higher production volume.

Fixed marketing expenses stay at $1,750,000, but the variable marketing expenses have increased from $62,500 to $312,500 for the Added Units column.

INCREMENTAL PROFITS WITH 2,500 ADDED UNITS

		Base Case	Added Units
Units		10,000	12,500
Sales price per unit		$1,000	$1,000
Total Revenues		$10,000,000	$12,500,000
Manufacturing Costs			
Variable per unit	$350	3,500,000	4,375,000
Fixed per unit		1,500,000	1,500,000
Total Manufacturing Costs		5,000,000	5,875,000
Research & Development Costs			
Variable per unit	$0	0	0
Fixed per unit		500,000	500,000
Total Research & Development Costs		500,000	500,000
Marketing Expenses			
Variable per unit	$25	250,000	312,500
Fixed per unit		1,750,000	1,750,000
Total Marketing Expenses		2,000,000	2,062,500
General and Administrative Expenses			
Variable per unit	$20	200,000	250,000
Fixed per unit		1,000,000	1,000,000
Total General and Admin. Expenses		1,200,000	1,250,000
Selling Costs			
Variable per unit	$30	300,000	375,000
Fixed per unit		900,000	900,000
Total Selling Costs		1,200,000	1,275,000

continues

Total Revenues	10,000,000	12,500,000
Total Variable Costs	4,250,000	5,312,500
Total Variable Costs per unit	425	425
Total Fixed Costs	5,650,000	5,650,000
Total Costs	9,900,000	10,962,500
Total Costs per unit	990	877
Operating Profit	100,000	1,537,500
Incremental Profit from 2,500 additional units		1,437,500

Exhibit 4.5   Incremental Profits

General and administrative expenses are dominated by fixed costs of $1,000,000 which do not change with the added volume, but the variable component of this expense category rises by $50,000 ($20 for each of the additional 2,500 units).

The fixed component of selling expenses stays at $900,000 but the variable component rises to $375,000 due to the added costs of selling the additional units.

The total fixed costs at the higher production level are unchanged from the 10,000 unit production level. Both cases show total fixed costs of $5,650,000. The total variable costs are higher, based on the incremental costs associated with making, selling, and delivering an extra 2,500 units. Total variable costs for the Added Units case equals $5,312,500. Instead of having total fixed and variable costs of $9,900,000, the Added Units case brings total fixed and variable costs to $10,962,500. When these total costs are subtracted from the total revenues from 12,500 units (10,000 Base Case units plus 2,500 Added units) the operating profit soars to $1,537,500. An additional 2,500 units, a 25 percent increase in sales, improved operating profits by a factor of 1,537.5. Just 2,500 additional units brought an additional $1,437,500 of profit to the bottom line.

Incremental profits can also be calculated as shown below:

Added Units	2,500
Price	$1,000
Incremental Revenues	$2,500,000
Incremental Revenues	$2,500,000
Incremental Expenses:	
Manufacturing @ $350 each	875,000
Research & Development	0
Marketing @ $25 each	62,500
General & Administrative @ $20 each	50,000
Selling @ $30 each	75,000
Total Incremental Expenses	1,062,500
Total Incremental Profit	$1,437,500

Now suppose that the variable cost portion of each expense category was improperly estimated. Suppose that fixed expenses were less than originally thought and variable expenses were higher than originally thought. In the Base Case, a reallocation of expenses between fixed and variable doesn't matter. Total expenses, fixed and variable, are still $9.9 million. When subtracted from total revenues of $10 million, operating profit is still $100,000 for the Base Case. But a substantial difference becomes evident when incremental profits are calculated. Exhibit 4.6 shows that a slight reallocation of expenses between fixed and variable classification reduces the incremental profits to $987,500.

With variable manufacturing costs at $400 per unit, variable marketing expenses at $80 per unit, variable general and administrative costs at $55 per unit, and variable selling costs at $70 per unit, Exhibit 4.6 shows that the incremental profit drops to $987,500. Thus, higher variable costs reduce incremental profits.

Conversely, higher fixed costs (lower variable costs) increase incremental profits. In the most extreme case, if all costs were fixed then the total variable costs for each additional unit would equal $0

INCREMENTAL PROFITS WITH 2,500 ADDED UNITS

		Base Case	Added Units
Units		10,000	12,500
Sales price per unit		$1,000	$1,000
Total Revenues		$10,000,000	$12,500,000
Manufacturing Costs			
Variable per unit	$400	4,000,000	5,000,000
Fixed per unit		1,000,000	1,000,000
Total Manufacturing Costs		5,000,000	6,000,000
Research & Development Costs			
Variable per unit	$0	0	0
Fixed per unit		500,000	500,000
Total Research & Development Costs		500,000	500,000
Marketing Expenses			
Variable per unit	$80	800,000	1,000,000
Fixed per unit		1,200,000	1,200,000
Total Marketing Expenses		2,000,000	2,200,000
General and Administrative Expenses			
Variable per unit	$55	550,000	687,500
Fixed per unit		650,000	650,000
Total General and Admin. Expenses		1,200,000	1,337,500
Selling Costs			
Variable per unit	$70	700,000	875,000
Fixed per unit		500,000	500,000
Total Selling Costs		1,200,000	1,375,000

continues

Total Revenues	10,000,000	12,500,000
Total Variable Costs	6,050,000	7,562,500
Total Variable Costs per unit	605	605
Total Fixed Costs	3,850,000	3,850,000
Total Costs	9,900,000	11,412,500
Total Costs per unit	990	913
Operating Profit	100,000	1,087,500
Incremental Profit from 2,500 additional units		987,500

Exhibit 4.6   Incremental Profits—
Revised Allocation of Fixed and Variable Costs

and the incremental profit for each unit would be equal to the selling price for each unit—$2,500. The entire selling price would fall to the bottom line. Detailed information from infringing financial managers and cost accountants is vital to defining a proper allocation of fixed and variable costs.

4.12   FIXED COSTS AREN'T ALWAYS FIXED

Fixed expenses only maintain their character within a certain range of sales volume. For example, at certain levels of sales volume, more manufacturing buildings will be needed. This entails more machinery, more administrative people for accounting, more insurance for the new buildings, more computers for the added records generated, larger work forces, and expanded layers of supervision. The theory of variable and fixed expenses is quite valid within certain boundaries of sales volume. However, once the limits are exceeded, the analysis can take on expanded complexities.

Economic recession may cause many companies to have overcapacity. In many cases, production volume can be increased by substantial amounts without adding much in the way of fixed costs. As economic activity increases the possibility exists that expenses generally characterized as fixed will need special attention.

4.13 SUMMARY

Lost profits are a function of volume, price, and costs. The character of expenses is very important for calculating lost profits. Understanding the nuances of fixed and variable expenses is important for making a lost-profit case. This chapter discussed the different expenses involved with business and categorized variable and fixed expenses. In this chapter an example of a lost-profit calculation provided a demonstration of the significant swing that can occur from misallocating variable and fixed expenses.

The following list reviews some of the major cases that have damage theory implications in intellectual property and particularly patent infringement cases. Important concepts and quotations from many of these cases appear in this and other chapters of the book. This list is intended to provide the advanced reader who wishes to review the case law with a road map of some of the seminal cases. The following is not intended to be a comprehensive list of all intellectual property cases with damage theory implications.

LIST OF INTELLECTUAL PROPERTY CASES WITH IMPORTANT DAMAGE THEORY IMPLICATIONS

- *Georgia-Pacific Corp. v. U.S. Plywood Corp.* 318 F. Supp. 1116, 6 USPQ 235 (S.D.N.Y. 1970)
- *Panduit Corp. v. Stahlin Brothers Fibre Works* 575 F2d 1152, 197 USPQ 726 (6th Cir. 1978)
- *State Industries Inc. v. Mor-Flo Industries Inc.* 883 F.2d 1573 (Fed. Cir. 1989)

- *BIC Leisure Products, Inc. et al. v. Windsurfing International, Inc.* 761 F. Supp. 1032, 19 USPQ 2d 1992 (S.D.N.Y. 1991)
- *Rite-Hite Corporation v. Kelley Company, Inc.,* 629 F. Supp. 1042, 231 USPQ 161 (E.D. Wis. 1986), 35 USPQ 2d 1065 (Fed. Cir. 1995)
- *King Instruments v. Perego* 737 F. Supp. 1227
- *Standard Havens Products, Inc. v. Gencor Industries Inc.* 953 F.2d 1360
- *Aro Manufacturing Co. v. Convertible Top Replacement Co.,* 377 US 476, 507, 141 USPQ 681, 694 (1964)
- *Minco Inc. v. Combustion Engineering* 95 F.3d 1109
- *Minnesota Mining & Mfg. Co. v. Johnson & Johnson Ortho-pedics, Inc.* 976 F.2d 1559
- *TWM Mfg. Co., Inc. v. Dura Corp.* 789 F.2d 895
- *Hartness International, Inc. v. Simplimatic Engineering Co.* 819 F.2d 1100
- *BASF Corp. v. Old World Trading Co.* 41 F.3d 1081
- *Gillette Co. v. Wilkinson Sword, Inc.* 1992 WL 30938
- *Waits v. Frito-Lay, Inc.* 978 F.2d 1093
- *U-Haul International Inc. v. Jartran Inc.* 793 F.2d 1034
- *ALPO Petfoods, Inc. v. Ralston-Purina Co.* 997 F.2d 949
- *Micro-Motio Inc. v. Exac Corp.* 19 USPQ 2d 1001
- *Pfizer Inc. v. International Rectifier Corporation et al.* 218 USPQ 586
- *2Pesos, Inc. v. Taco Cabana* 505 U.S. 763
- *Livesay Window Co. v. Livesay Industries, Inc.,* 251 F.2d 469, 471–72, 116 USPQ 167, 168–70 (5th Cir. 1958)
- *Lessona Corp. v. United States* 599 F.2d 958, 202 USPQ 414, 439 (Ct. C. 1981)
- *Lam, Inc. v. Johns-Manville Corp.* 718 F.2d 1056, 219 USPQ 670 (Fed. Cir. 1983)
- *King Instrument Corp. v. Otari Corp.* 767 F.2d 853, 226 USPQ 402 (Fed. Cir. 1985)

- *Bio-Rad Laboratories, Inc. v. Nicolet Instrument Corporation* 739 F.2d 604, 222 USPQ 654 (Fed. Cir.) cert. Denied, 469 U.S. 1038 (1984)
- *Fonar Corp. v. General Electric Co.* 107 F.3d 1543; 902 F. Supp. 330; 118 S. Ct. 266
- *Merrill Hebert v. Lisle Corp.* 99 F.3d 1109 (1996)

5

Royalty Rates and the Georgia-Pacific Factors

When infringement has been shown, a patentee is entitled to "damages adequate to compensate for the infringement, but in no event less than a reasonable royalty for the use made of the invention by the infringer." 35 U.S.C. § 284 (1994). In *Stickle v Heublein, Inc.*, the court said, "The amount of the royalty should be that amount which adequately compensates for the infringement.[1]

In *Georgia-Pacific Corp. v. United States Plywood Corp.*,[2] the court listed fifteen factors that it considered important for deriving a reasonable royalty. These factors have been widely adopted for use in reasonable royalty determination. These factors are typically considered in the context of the patentee and infringer engaging in a hypothetical negotiation for a license of the patent in suit. The fifteen factors listed by the court are listed and discussed in this chapter.[3]

5.1 FACTORS FOR DERIVING A RESPONSIBLE ROYALTY

(1) The royalties received by the patentee for the licensing of the patent in suit, proving or tending to prove an established royalty.

When the patentee has licensed the patent in suit to others, very useful information is provided about the rate that might be used for calculating

---

[1] See *Stickle v. Heublein, Inc.*, 716 F.2d 1550, 1562, 219 USPQ2d 377, 386 (Fed. Cir. 1983)

[2] *Georgia-Pacific Corp. v. United States Plywood Corp.*, 318 F. Supp. 1116 (S.D.N.Y. 1970), *modified*, 446 F.2d 295 (2d Cir. 1970), *cert. denied*, 404 U.S. 870 (1971).

[3] The District Court in Georgia-Pacific indicated that in theory, "there is no formula by which these factors can be rated precisely in order of their relative importance."

damages. In some cases one license can be enough to establish a royalty rate for the patent in suit. Some industries have limited participants. A license given to only one of them can sometimes show the value of the patent in suit. Other times, more licenses are required to cause a royalty rate to be considered as established.

The Federal Circuit remarked that in order to establish a royalty rate, it must be paid by such a number of persons "as to indicate a general acquiescence in its reasonableness." *Hanson v. Alpine Valley Ski Area, Inc.*, 718 F.2d 1075, 1078 (Fed. Cir. 1983), quoting *Rude v. Westcott*, 130 U.S. 152, 165 (1889).

Royalty rates that were negotiated during settlement of actual or threatened litigation are mostly discounted because their licensing rates may have been influenced more by the desire to avoid litigation costs than by the true value the parties placed on the invention. (*Panduit Corp. v. Stahlin Bros. Fibre Works, Inc.*, 575 F.2d 1152, 1164 n. 11 (6th Cir. 1978)). Such license agreements are not necessarily admissible under Rule 408 of the Federal Rules of Evidence, which provides: Evidence of (1) furnishing or offering or promising to furnish, or (2) accepting or offering or promising to accept, a valuable consideration in compromise or attempting to compromise a claim which was disputed as to either validity or amount, is not admissible to prove liability for or invalidity of the claim or its amount. Evidence of conduct made in compromise negotiations is likewise not admissible.

Sometimes a history of licensing can be impaired by infringement. In *Susan Maxwell v. J. Baker, Inc.* the instructions to the jury included the following, "Maxwell contends that she was forced to offer licenses based on a diminished royalty because she felt that there was a widespread and open disregard of her patent rights. J. Baker, on the other hand, contends that the patent had not been disregarded and that Maxwell's offers were consistent with her existing marketing program. If you should find that the disregard of the patent forced Maxwell to seek a decreased royalty, you may determine that the rate offered by Maxwell was not a true measure of a reasonable royalty."

In this instance the court indicated that a license containing a royalty rate offered to others in an industry might not be considered an established rate.

Even when the patents in suit have been licensed and royalty rates have been paid by third parties, additional analysis is sometimes needed to give great weight to the royalty rates that address this factor.

(2) The rates paid by the licensee for the use of other patents comparable to the patent in suit.

In addition to the rates paid by the licensee for other patents, the rates paid by other industry participants for comparable patents can be a useful indication of the royalty rate for calculating damages. Royalty rates paid only by the hypothetical licensee can be too limiting and this limitation seems to serve no useful purpose. The hypothetical licensee may not have licensed any other patents while others in the industry may be active licensees. Similar patented technology that is licensed by independent third-parties for use in the same industry can have relevance for determining a royalty rate for the patents in suit.

(3) The nature and scope of the license, as exclusive or non-exclusive; or as restricted or non-restricted in terms of territory or with respect to whom the manufactured product may be sold.

This factor can be interpreted to require that the concluded royalty rate for damages should reflect characteristics of the license that they would be expected to negotiate. When analyzing the licenses referred to in factors 1 and 2, the nature of the licenses should also be considered. Most often the basis for a reasonable royalty rate is non-exclusive.

A non-exclusive license may not be appropriate for the damages calculation where the hypothetical licensor and licensee would negotiate an exclusive agreement. Typically, exclusive licenses involve a higher royalty rate than non-exclusive licenses. This observation, however, is difficult to quantitatively support. A comparison of the rate at which a patent is licensed under an exclusive agreement to the rate at which the same patent is licensed non-exclusively is not usually possible. One licensing instance however does provide support for this contention. The following story was reported in a past issue of *Licensing Economics Review*.

> Molecular Biosystems, Inc. (MBI) announced that it has amended its supply and license agreement with E. I. du Pont De Nemours & Company which covers proprietary nucleic acid probe technologies that are owned by MBI. The recently renegotiated agreement was originally established in April 1986. Previously du Pont had an exclusive license, but under the new agreement, will only retain a non-exclusive right to these technologies. MBI will continue to manufacture nucleic acid probe agents for du Pont as it did under the previous agreement. The royalty rate on du Pont's net sales was lowered from 5.5% to 4% to reflect the change of du Pont's licensing rights from exclusive to non-exclusive. This represents a reduction in the royalty rate of 27%.
>
> Vincent A. Frank, President and Chief Executive Officer of MBI said "The new structure enables MBI to maximize the potential of its market opportunities while, at the same time, custom tailoring MBI's relationship with du Pont to best fulfill the needs of both companies."[4]

Generally non-exclusive license agreements serve as the basis for addressing this factor.

---

[4] *Licensing Economics Review*, March 1991, page 4.

(4) **The licensor's established policy and marketing program to maintain its patent monopoly by not licensing others to use the invention or by gaining licenses under special conditions designed to preserve that monopoly.**

A higher royalty rate can be justified when this condition is met. A formal written policy does not usually exist but this condition can be established by considering the actions of the patentee with regard to the number and type of licenses they typically negotiate. The implication of this factor, in some cases, means that the patent holder would not license the patents in suit under any conditions. The Georgia-Pacific factors, however, force a hypothetical negotiation between the parties in the suit. A conflict between the actual negotiating posture of the patentee and the hypothetical negotiation is created by this factor. This dilemma will be discussed more fully under factor 15.

(5) **The commercial relationship between the licensor and the licensee, such as, whether they are competitors in the same territory in the same line of business; or whether they are inventor and promoter.**

This factor has caused significant debate. The knee-jerk reaction to this factor typically leads to a conclusion that an inventor (patentee) that is dealing with a company would settle for a lower royalty rate than if the patentee were an industry participant. The reason cited is that the inventor is not in a position to make or sell a patented product and as such has less negotiating leverage. A more detailed analysis can sometimes bring this reaction into question. If the patent is useful to only one company then an inventor may find itself in a limited bargaining position. When several companies compete in an industry the inventor has a better bargaining position. The inventor can use the corporate competitors against each other to gain a bargaining advantage. This can be viewed as eliminating the fact that the inventor cannot compete, thereby allowing the inventor to gain the maximum royalty rate possible. Consideration should also be given to the goals and objectives of an inventor. Many companies engage in research and licensing for their livelihood. Just because they do not manufacture and sell products does not mean that they are likely to negotiate sub-standard royalty rates. In fact, they are interested in maximizing their profits from inventing by obtaining the highest royalty rate possible. Such companies are not likely to negotiate a substandard royalty rate because they are not industry participants. As such, this factor can lead to a knee-jerk reaction that is sometimes inappropriate.

(6) The effect of selling the patented specialty in promoting sales of other products of the licensee; the existing value of the invention to the licensor as a generator of sales of its non-patented items; and the extent of such derivative or convoyed sales.

This factor addresses the instances where some patented products generate sales of other company products that are not covered by the patent. To the extent that this is true, the concluded royalty rate should reflect this factor. Marketing materials of the infringer often discuss this factor when convoyed sales are expected. Sometimes budgets and planning documents show specific sales increases for convoyed sales.

In *Deere & Co. v. Int'l Harvester Co.,* 710 F.2d 1554, 1558-1559 (Fed. Cir. 1983), the lower court, in determining a reasonable royalty, explained that the sales of the patented product facilitated sales of a more important and more profitable machine (collateral items). According to the district court, in considering the importance of the collateral products, the infringer would have paid a substantial percentage of its net sales on the infringing product as a royalty, "even exceeding its expected profit on [its infringing corn heads], to protect [the collateral non-infringing product's] sales and profits."

For more information, refer to *Deere & Co. v. International Harvester Co.,* 218 USPQ 403, 407 (C.D. Ill. 1982). The Federal Circuit affirmed.

(7) The duration of the patent and the term of the license.

This factor is not always as important as you might think. A long patent life can leave a licensee with few options for using the patented invention. Waiting for expiration of the patent may force the licensee to be out of the market for too long. This can have disastrous consequences to a strategic plan. In such cases a such, a high royalty rate may be warranted. At the same time, a high royalty may be acceptable where a short patent life exists. A licensee may find a high royalty rate acceptable for a short period of time until the patent expires. In this instance, the licensee can stay in the market without having to agree to a high long-term expense in the form of a royalty rate.

(8) The established profitability of the product made under the patent; its commercial success; and its current popularity.

Established profitability may not exist for some infringing products. Early in the life cycle of products, profits can be sacrificed to gain market share. Huge advertising expenses can eliminate profits during the initial introduction of a patented product. Such expenditures are usually spent to capture market share. Later, the advertising and promotional expenses are reduced and profits can become substantial. As such, a patented product may not have an established level of profits but can still be valuable and still deserve a high royalty rate. In other cases sales reports or consumer research can demonstrate the commercial success and current popularity of a patented product. Such information should be viewed in the context of the industry and market niches that the product serves. A few thousand units of sales can be a great success for some products, but a disaster for other types of products.

(9)   The utility and advantage of the patent property over the old modes or devices, if any, that had been used for working out similar results.

Technical information is the first place to look for addressing this factor but consumer research can also provide clues about the superiority of the patented product over previous versions. In some instances, the patented property is an incremental improvement over an older method or device. A differential profit calculation can provide a possible indication of a reasonable royalty rate. The difference between the profits of the product (or other commercial exploitation) before the patented invention was introduced and the product profits afterward can indicate a reasonable royalty rate. This can be especially true where a patented invention has been used to improve a continuous process.

(10)   The nature of the patented invention; the character of the commercial embodiment of it as owned and produced by the licensor; and the benefits to those who have used the invention.

This factor is often addressed by considering the patented invention with respect to its overall commercialization. Is it a stand-alone product or is it part of a larger item? Higher royalties can sometimes be associated with product-defining inventions as opposed to inventions that simply add enhancements to existing products. However, this does not necessarily mean that an enhancing feature should command a low royalty rate where the feature can be shown to have caused higher sales or profits for the improved product.

(11)   The extent to which the infringer has made use of the invention; and any evidence probative of the value of that use.

Evidence that supports this factor can be wide-ranging. Sales, profits, convoyed sales, stock price increases, and other economic benefits can sometimes be attributed to the patents in suit. Many of these possibilities are specifically addressed by other Georgia-Pacific factors. Areas not specially covered can be introduced by this factor. In some cases the patent in suit can simply improve a company's prestige. Prestige alone may not be directly profitable, but an improved image in the eyes of customers can have an overall benefit to the company. One caveat—the degree to which this exists can sometimes be difficult to quantify.

(12)   The portion of the profit or selling price that may be customary in the particular business or in comparable businesses to allow for the use of the invention or analogous inventions.

Rarely do customary profit allocations exist for an industry. Some industries have vague rules-of-thumb but they are seldom directly applicable to a specific case. Most of the time, the information derived from considering the other factors dominate.

(13)   The portion of the realizable profit that should be credited to the invention as distinguished from non-patented elements, the manufacturing process, business risks, or significant features or improvements added by the infringer.

A reasonable royalty would typically allow for profits to be attributed to earning a return on other assets used in commercializing the infringing product. Instances can exist, however, where all profits might be paid as a royalty because of other economic benefits that a licensee expects from use of the invention (see previous discussion on convoyed sales). The Analytical Approach can be useful in addressing this factor as can an investment rate of return analysis. This factor allows for profits to be earned by the infringer after allowing for the reasonable royalty rate.

(14) The opinion and testimony of qualified experts.

This factor is pertinent to the court and/or jury and is presented by the report and testimony of an expert.

(15) The amount that a licensor (such as the patentee) and a licensee (such as the infringer) would have agreed upon (at the time the infringement began) if both had been reasonably and voluntarily trying to reach an agreement; that is, that amount which a prudent licensee—who desires, as a business proposition, to obtain a license to manufacture and sell a particular article embodying the patented invention—would have been willing to pay as a royalty and yet be able to make a reasonable profit and which amount would have been acceptable by a prudent patentee who was willing to grant a license.

This factor is the basis for considering the information collected to address the previous 14 factors. In coming to a reasonable royalty rate conclusion the question becomes, "What royalty rate would the two parties in suit come to if they were sincerely trying to reach a license agreement and had the information available to them that addresses the previous 14 factors." The answer to this question establishes an indication of a reasonable royalty rate to use for calculating damages.

Underlying assumptions are imposed on the negotiating parties about the patents in suit and the allegedly infringing commercial activity. The first assumption has to do with validity of the patents. The hypothetical negotiators are to negotiate with the understanding that both parties know for certain that the patents in suit are valid and enforceable. This is unlike a license negotiation that occurs outside the context of an infringement lawsuit. Typically, negotiating parties may spend a great deal of time and effort arguing over the validity and enforceability of the patents to be licensed. Such negotiations can sometimes result in a compromise that is addressed by a lower royalty rate. The second assumption imposed on the negotiation has to do with the commercial activity that initiated the suit. The negotiators are to negotiate with the understanding that both parties know for certain that the commercial activity of the defendant infringes the patents in suit. This is also unlike a license negotiation that occurs outside the context of an infringement lawsuit. Typically, the negotiators spend great time and effort arguing about the commercial activity and whether it actually infringes the subject of the licensing negotiations. Even if the parties agree that the patents are valid and enforceable, the licensee may have strong arguments that bring infringement into question. Here, too, such negotiations can sometimes result in a compromise that is addressed by a lower royalty rate. For the Georgia-Pacific hypothetical negotiation these elements of the negotiation are established and not open for interpretation.

Typically the negotiation is assumed to take place at the date when infringement first began. This usually means the date at which commercial exploitation of the infringed property started. So, the hypothetical licensor and licensee are assumed to be voluntarily locked in a room with information that addresses the first 14 factors. A rigid interpretation of this scenario suggests that the information to be used by the negotiating parties is limited to that which was available at the time of the hypothetical negotiation. In this scenario, the parties would be assumed to negotiate at the date of first infringement using only information that would be available at the date of first infringement. Under this scenario if high sales growth, huge profits and dominant market share were not realized from exploitation of the infringed property until years after the first infringing sales, then this information would not be considered as part of the negotiation. Very often infringement lawsuits take place years after the first date of infringement and much information becomes available that might not have been available at the hypothetical negotiation date. Many of the answers to the 14 previously discussed factors could be different depending on the date of the negotiation. As an example, profit expectations that might have existed at the hypothetical negotiation date may have been long ago proved as incorrect. Or, active licensing of the patent in suit may have been accomplished since infringement began. In fact, an established royalty rate may actually exist by the trial date but not at the time of the hypothetical negotiation. Many courts have addressed this problem by allowing the use of information that became available after the date at which the hypothetical negotiation takes place. In one case, information about actual profits was allowed for consideration (*Deere & Co. v. International Harcester Co.,* 710 F2.d 1555, 1558 (Fed. Cir. 1983)). Such information is allowed into the negotiation if the parties could have reasonably anticipated it at the time of the hypothetical negotiation date. Of course this can lead to arguments about what information could have been reasonably anticipated and what information was beyond the imagination of the negotiating parties. Recently, this problem was addressed by allowing all information to be used in the hypothetical negotiation.

In *Susan Maxwell v. J. Baker* the jury instructions included the following statement by the court, "In determining a reasonable royalty, you are to imagine that a hypothetical negotiation took place between J. Baker and Maxwell at or about the time that J. Baker first infringed the patent. You must assume that Maxwell was willing to grant a license and that J. Baker was willing to accept one. . . . In determining the result of such a hypothetical negotiation, you may consider facts and events that occurred after the alleged infringement began, even though they would not have been known to the parties at the time of the hypothetical negotiation. . . . ."[5] This instruction allowed for all information to be used in the negotiation, regardless of whether it could have been anticipated by the negotiating parties.

Many argue that the patentee would not offer a license under any circumstances and that this underlying assumption is unrealistic. Nonetheless, the framework established under Georgia-Pacific insists that the two parties to the suit be hypothetically placed in a situation where they must come to terms under which the plaintiff would have licensed the infringed property to the defendant. This can conflict with the information that addresses factor 4. Instances exist where the patentee claims that a license would not have been granted under any circumstances, yet factor 15 forces a hypothetical negotiation. Reconciliation can only be accomplished by giving considerable weight to the patentees position (as addressed by factor 4) and concluding a higher royalty rate than might otherwise be concluded. Evidence to support an economic advantage for the patentee from taking this position is important to support an upward royalty rate conclusion.

5.2 SUMMARY

The Georgia-Pacific factors provide a framework for determining a royalty rate for use in calculating damages. Not all of the factors provide exact quantification of an answer but they are an excellent starting point for qualifying the value of the patent in suit.

The Georgia-Pacific factors are fundamental to establishing a reasonable royalty rate. Other methods are useful for refining the final answer but these fifteen factors are the traditional starting point for royalty rate-base damages.

---

[5] United States Court of Appeals for the Federal Circuit, 95-1292,-1293,-1355, *Susan M. Maxwell v. J. Baker, Inc.*

6

The
Analytical Approach

The analytical approach is a method for deriving a reasonable royalty. It has characteristics that can lead to an appropriate conclusion. The analytical approach determines a reasonable royalty as the difference between profits expected from infringing sales and a normal industry profit level. The analytical approach can be summarized by the following equation:

$$\text{Expected Profit Margin} - \text{Normal Profit Margin} = \text{Royalty Rate}$$
$$\text{(Eq. 6.1)}$$

In TWM Mfg. Co., Inc. v. Dura Corp., 789 F.2d 895, 899 (Fed. Cir. 1986), a royalty rate for damages was calculated based on an analysis of the business plan of the infringer prepared just prior to the onset of the infringing activity. The court discovered the profit expectations of the infringer from internal memorandums written by top executives of the company. Internal memorandums showed that company management expected to earn gross profit margins of almost 53 percent from the proposed infringing sales. Operating profit margins were then calculated by subtracting overhead costs to yield an expected profit margin of between 37 percent and 42 percent. To find the portion of this profit level that should be provided as a royalty to the plaintiff, the court considered the normal profits earned in the industry at the time of infringement. These profit levels were determined to be between 6.6 percent and 12.5 percent. These normal industry profits were considered to represent profit margins that would be acceptable to firms operating in the industry. The remaining 30 percent of profits were found to represent a reasonable royalty from which to calculate infringement damages. On appeal, the Federal Circuit affirmed.

An important characteristic of this royalty method, as used by the court for this case, is the emphasis placed on the profit expectations associated with using the intellectual property at the time of the infringement. Actual profits realized during infringement were decided to be irrelevant in this case. If instead of infringing, a royalty had been negotiated as part of a license, the licensee would have considered the amount they expected to earn from exploiting the intellectual property while negotiating the amount of royalty they would be willing to pay. The focus of negotiations would be on profit expectations. Actual profits would not be considered because actual profits would not have been earned since sales activities would not have begun at the time of the negotiations. Some courts allow profitability information after the date of infringement to be introduced as a consideration for determining a reasonable royalty, as previously discussed in Chapter 5.

Another important characteristic of the analytical approach is the search for a benchmark level of earnings that infringers should be allowed to keep before any excess profits are allocated to the intellectual property owner. Unlike a lost-profit calculation, a reasonable royalty allows some level of profits to remain with the infringer/licensee.

6.1 NORMAL INDUSTRY PROFITS

A difficulty with the analytical approach centers on answering the question, "What is normal?" Many companies in the same industry, offering the same types of products to the same types of customers, can show wide swings in profit margins. Presented are the net profit margins for six companies that compete in the same industry, selling similar products to similar types of customers. The profit margins range from a low of 0.2 percent to a high of 11.4 percent. The average for the six companies is 6.5 percent. The average increases to 9.4 percent if Beauicontrol Cosmetics and Helene Curtis are eliminated from the average.

Cosmetics Companies

Company	Profit Margin
Aloette Cosmetics	8.2%
Avon Products	8.6%
Beauticontrol Cosmetics	0.2%
DEP Corporation	9.4%
Helene Curtis	1.2%
Jean Philippe Fragrances	11.4%

It can also be difficult to find agreement on what constitutes normal profit margins for an individual company. Different subsidiaries, divisions, and even different product lines within the same company can display wide swings in profitability. Many large companies have a portfolio of businesses. Some of the product offerings are mature products which enjoy large market shares but contribute only moderate profit margins because of selling price competition. Other product offerings are emerging products that have great potential for profits and market share but won't deliver earnings contribution until a later date. Still other products of the same diversified company might contribute huge profits because of a technological advantage but only from exploitation of a small market niche. Shown below are the annual earnings from three different products of a hypothetical company called Diversified Company.

Diversified Company Product Line Profitability
(millions)

Product Offering	Annual Sales	Total Earnings	Profit Margin
Mature Product	$1,429	$86	6%
High Tech Product	516	77	15%
Emerging Product	333	10	3%
Total	$2,278	$173	7.6%

The overall profitability of the company is 7.6 percent, calculated as the total earnings of $173 million divided by the total sales of $2.278 billion. The overall profitability of the company may not be appropriate for use as a normal industry profit margin for any one of the individual product lines. Each product line shows profit margins that are very different from the profitability of the overall company. Even use of the individual profit margins can be inappropriate. In the case of the Emerging Product, the low profit margin may be the result of continued research and aggressive marketing. These early stage expenses drain current profitability but will hopefully be recouped from higher profits in the future. As such, the normal industry profits for the Emerging Product will not be defined until much later.

It has been argued that the overall profitability of the company represents the normal amount that should be used in the analytical approach. Such a practice would unfairly penalize a company that practices diversification. Suppose that Diversified Company infringed the patents of another company with a product in its High Tech Product category. Suppose further that the infringing product delivered a profit margin of 20 percent. Using the 15 percent profit margin as the industry standard would leave a royalty award of 5 percent for the plaintiff, but using the overall company profit of 7.6 percent would raise the royalty rate to 12.4 percent. Diversified Company would be inappropriately penalized for practicing diversification. If they had never started the other two product lines then the royalty rate award would be the lower 5 percent. Careful analysis is required to properly use the analytical approach.

The analytical approach can be very useful. It is based on information timely to the infringement. It attempts to allocate the profits earned from intellectual property exploitation between the infringer and infringed. Unlike a lost-profit calculation, a reasonable royalty would leave the infringer, at least in a licensing context, with some sort of profit adequate to compensate the infringer for business investment and risks. The analytical approach is especially useful if a normalized standard industry profit can be properly derived; this can be difficult but not impossible. The analytical approach can provide an order of magnitude indication of a reasonable royalty. The analytical approach can be improved, however.

6.2 A MORE COMPREHENSIVE ANALYTICAL APPROACH

Missing from the analytical approach is consideration of the amount of complementary assets required for exploitation of the subject intellectual property. A unique intellectual property might require significantly more investment in manufacturing assets than is typical for an industry. As such, the industry standard profit margin might be inappropriate. From another viewpoint, the industry profit requirement for commercializing specific intellectual property requiring massive fixed asset investment might be higher than the profits typically required in a specific industry. This could easily happen if new intellectual property is being introduced into an industry not accustomed to capital-intensive activities.

The analytical approach loses sight of the balance sheet. Profits are important but they are not independent of investment in complementary business assets. Otherwise everyone with an idea would be in business. The profit and loss statement is derived from the management of the investment in the assets reported on the balance sheet. Exploitation of intellectual property requires the integration of different types of resources and assets. Intellectual property by itself rarely spews forth money. The equation of commercialization requires working capital, fixed assets, intangible assets, and intellectual property as previously discussed. A more comprehensive version of the analytical approach can sometimes be utilized, enhanced to the extent that the profits to be allocated between the infringer and infringed reflect the dynamic relationship between profits and the amounts invested in the complementary assets. When balance sheet information is available an investment rate of return analysis (discussed in Chapter 7) can be used to support the royalty rate derived from the analytical approach.

6.3 HYPOTHETICAL EXAMPLE

Presented in Exhibit 6.1 are the profit margin expectations of Exciting Biotech, Inc. associated with commercialization of a new patented drug therapy. By subtracting the enhanced operating profit margins from an industry *norm*, the portion of profits that can be attributed to proprietary technology are isolated as a royalty rate.

Presented in Exhibit 6.2 are the operating profit margins for a group of generic drug companies that arguably are producing commodity products. The products are competitively priced, mass produced, widely distributed, and provide their makers with slim profit margins in comparison to proprietary products. The profit margins were derived from information downloaded from the Disclosure database on public corporations via CompuServe. Adjustments were incorporated into the operating profit margins to attempt to isolate the profits derived

US New Product Revenue Forecast—1996
Exciting Biotech, Inc.
($millions)

	1996	1997	1998	1999	2000	2001	2002	2003	2004	2005
Primary Market Revenues	0	0	100	300	400	550	600	625	650	675
Net Income Before Tax	−25	0	80	150	225	350	375	385	395	400
Profit Margin	deficit	0%	80%	50%	56%	64%	63%	62%	61%	59%

Average Profit Margin 98-05   62%

Exhibit 6.1   Exciting Biotech, Inc. Profit Margin Expectations

Generic Drug Company
Average Operating Profit Margins

Company	Profit Margin	Period Averaged
Barr Labs	10.50%	90–95
Biocraft Labs	10.70%	89–95
Copley Pharmaceuticals	38.60%	89–94
VAX Corp.	15.20%	89–94
Mylan Labs	31.20%	89–95
Pharmaceutical Resources	16.00%	92–94
Purepac nc.	28.00%	91–94
Watson Pharmaceuticals	34.00%	89–94
Group Average	**23.03%**	

The group average gives equal weight to each company average. Company averages are not weighted by volume.

Operating profit margins were calculated as: net sales *minus* cost of goods sold and selling and administration expenses, *before* research and development and interest expenses.

The primary source of the financial information used to calculate the profit margins was the Disclosure computer database accessed through Compuserve.

The average operating profit margins reported above were calculated for the years indicated in column 3 to reflect profits most relevant to the hypothetical negotiation date. The periods selected were based on the availability of data and the adjustment of loss years in order to reflect a normalized level of profits for each generic drug company.

The average for Barr Labs reflects adjustments for elimination of profits associated with the Tamoxifen product and costs associated with non-recurring events.

The average for IVAX reflects adjustments for eliminating non-drug product lines.

The average for Pharmaceutical Resources excludes years prior to 1992 due to losses associated with restructuring Par Pharmaceuticals.

Information about the profits of Purepac, Inc. prior to 1991 are not meaningful because the company was in a start-up mode.

Exhibit 6.2   Operating Profits for Generic Drug Companies

from the operations of the selected companies. Adjustments were made to eliminate income and expenses associated with nonoperating assets and nonrecurring events when possible. Interest expenses were also eliminated. As a group, the average profit margins of these companies can be looked at as the commodity profit margin for the generic drug industry. In this case we have looked to estimate a *normal* or *commodity* profit margin by looking at the operating profit margins of companies in the business of manufacturing and selling generic drugs. The operating profit margins of several large generic drug manufacturers are presented in Exhibit 6.2. The profit margins of the companies are derived from participation in the drug industry without the benefit of patent protection.

The Analytical Approach indicates a royalty rate of 39 percent as calculated by subtracting the 23 percent generic drug company profit margin from the 62 percent profit margin expected by Exciting Biotech, Inc. from commercialization of the new proprietary invention.

6.4 GENERIC DRUG PRICING

Additional information that supports this level of royalty rate is developed from considering the price differential between proprietary drugs under patent protection and the same product sold as a generic drug after patent protection expires. The primary difference is the loss of patent protection. The following information indicates the enormous value of patent protection.

In a story about drug pricing, *Business Week* reported that the patent protection for the ulcer drug Tagamet is about to expire and "Mylan Laboratories is planning a clone of Tagamet for half the price."[1]

---

[1]"A Big Dose of Uncertainty—An industry plagued by high costs faces health-care reform," *Business Week*, January 10, 1994, p. 85.

This represents a 50 percent discount off the price of the product while under patent protection. In the same story *Business Week* said "Gross margins for generics are 50 percent to 60 percent, vs. 90 percent to 95 percent for branded products. . . ." The profit differential indicates a royalty rate under The Analytical Approach of between 30 percent to 45 percent.[2]

Business Week also discussed a new strategy being followed by the proprietary drug companies.[3] Faced with huge market share losses when a proprietary drug loses patent protection, these companies are introducing their own versions of generic copies of their proprietary drugs. *Business Week* said, "The majors often price generics at only 10 percent to 25 percent less than the brand-name price, while generics ideally should be half [50 percent] the full price.

Forbes reported that patent protection for Naprosyn, a $500 million (1992 annual sales) arthritis drug made by Syntex expired in December 1993.[4] Prior to the loss of patent protection the company introduced in October 1993 a generic version of the drug to try to ease the loss of its market share. A few months after the launch of Syntex's generic version, five other generic drug companies entered the market. Forbes said, "Soon the generics were selling at one-tenth [10 percent] of Naprosyn and had over 80 percent of the market." A royalty rate of 90 percent is indicated by this information.

Pharmaceutical Business News, a medical and health industry publication, reported, "Generic drugs typically cost 30 percent to 50 percent less than their brand-name counterparts."[5]

---

[2] Ibid.

[3] "The Drugmakers vs. The Trustbusters," *Business Week*, September 5, 1994, p. 67.

[4] "Drug wars," *Forbes*, August 29, 1994, p. 81.

[5] "Market forces usher in a golden age of generic drugs," *Pharmaceutical Business News*, November 29, 1993, published by Financial Times Business Information, Ltd., London, UK.

Chemical Marketing Reporter, a pharmaceutical industry publication, reported, "Industry analysts agree that brands will continue to be new drug innovators and generics will provide off-patent copies at one-fifth [20 percent] to one-half of the price [50 percent]."[6]

6.5 SUMMARY

The analytical approach is a viable model for deriving a royalty rate, but in many cases it should be used with other models to obtain support for the answer it provides.

---

[6]"Into the mainstream (greater cooperation between generic drug and name-brand drug makers)," *Chemical Marketing Reporter*, March 9, 1992, Schnell Publishing Company, Inc.

7

Investment Returns
and Royalty Rates

This chapter presents an approach for determining a royalty rate based on investment rate of returns. This analysis requires consideration of the profits expected from exploitation of the various assets of a business including the technology that has been infringed. Based on the business enterprise framework and an allocation of a fair rate of return to all of the integrated assets of a business, including the licensed technology, a fair rate of return for use of a specific patent can be derived and expressed as a royalty rate.

The basic principles in this type of analysis involve looking at the total profits of a business and allocating the profits among the different classes of assets used in the business. When a business demonstrates an ability to earn profits above that which would be expected from operating a commodity-oriented company, then the presence of intellectual property, such as patented technology, is identified. An allocation of the total profits derived from using all assets of the company can attribute a portion of the profits to the technology of a business. When the profits attributed to technology are expressed as a percentage of revenues, royalty rate guidance is obtained.

The investment rate of return analysis yields an indication of a royalty rate for a technology license after a fair return is earned on investment in the other assets of the business. Thus, a royalty rate conclusion that is supported by an investment rate of return analysis allows for payment of a royalty to a licensor while still allowing a licensee to earn a fair investment rate of return on its own non-licensed assets that are used in the business.

7.1 INVESTMENT RATE OF RETURN AND ROYALTY RATES

This method is based on the idea of allocating the total earnings of a technologically-based business among the different asset categories employed by the business. Exhibit 7.1 starts with the concepts introduced as the business enterprise framework and adds notations that will be used in the following paragraphs to develop the method.

The earnings of a business are derived from exploiting its assets. The amount of assets in each category along with the nature of the assets and their quality determines the level of earnings that the business generates. Working capital, fixed assets, and intangible assets are generally commodity types of assets that all businesses can possess and exploit. As previously discussed, a company that possesses only these limited assets will enjoy only limited amounts of earnings because of the competitive nature of commodity-dominated businesses.

A company that generates superior earnings must have something special—intellectual property in the form of patented technology, trademarks, or copyrights. The distribution of the earnings among the assets is primarily driven by the value of the assets and the investment risk of the assets. The total earnings of the company (T_e) as expressed below,

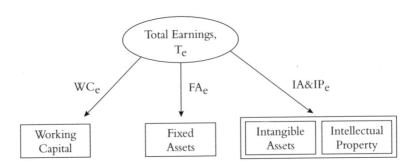

Exhibit 7.1   Distribution of Earnings

are comprised of earnings derived from use of working capital (WC_e), earnings derived from use of fixed assets (FA_e) and earnings derived from use of intangible assets and intellectual property ($IA\&IP_e$).

$$T_e = WC_e + FA_e + IA\&IP_e \qquad \text{(Eq. 7.1)}$$

The earnings associated with use of intangible assets and intellectual property are represented by $IA\&IP_e$. This level of earnings can be further subdivided into earnings associated with the use of the intangible assets (IA_e) and earnings associated with the use of intellectual property (IP_e) as shown below:

$$IA\&IP_e = IA_e + IP_e \qquad \text{(Eq. 7.2)}$$

7.2 ROYALTY RATES

An appropriate royalty rate is equal to the portion of IP_e that can be attributed to the use of the subject technology. The royalty rate to associate with a specific technology equals the earnings derived from the technology divided by the revenues derived with the technology as shown in Exhibit 7.2. Specifically, a company lacking intangible assets and technology would be reduced to operating a commodity-oriented enterprise where competition and lack of product distinction would severely limit the potential for profits. Conversely, a company possessing proprietary assets can throw off the restrictions of commodity-oriented operations and earn superior profits.

$$\frac{\text{Earnings Attributed to Technology}}{\text{Revenues}} = \text{Royalty Rate} \qquad \text{(Eq. 7.3)}$$

When a portion of the profit stream of a company is attributed to the proprietary assets of that company, an indication of the profits contributed by the existence of the proprietary assets is provided, and

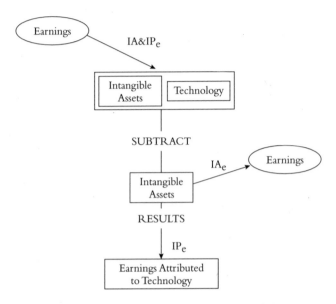

Exhibit 7.2   Excess Earnings as a Percent of Revenues

a basis for a royalty is established when the attributed profits are expressed as a percentage of the corresponding revenues. The total profits can be allocated among the different asset categories based on the amount of assets in each category and the relative investment risk associated with each asset category.

7.3   EXAMPLE COMPANY, INC.

Shown in Exhibit 7.3 is an allocation of the weighted average cost of capital[1] for an example business enterprise allocated among the business assets used in the business enterprise. The various rates of return

---

[1] The weighted average cost of capital is an investment rate of return required from business investments that is a weighting of the rates of return required by debt and equity investors. More information about this topic can be obtained from Appendix A.

assigned to each of the assets reflect their relative risk. The relative returns provided by each asset category is also indicated.

The monetary assets of the business are its net working capital. This is the total of current assets minus current liabilities. Current assets are comprised of accounts receivable, inventories, cash, and short term security investments. Offsetting this total are the current liabilities of the business such as accounts payable, accrued salaries, and accrued expenses. The value of this asset category can usually be taken directly from a company balance sheet. In this example, $10 million is invested in this asset category.

Working capital is considered to be the most liquid asset of a business. Receivables are usually collected within 60 days and inventories are usually turned over in 90 days. The cash component is immediately available and security holdings can be converted to cash with a telephone call to the firm's broker. Further evidence of liquidity is the use of accounts receivable and/or inventories as collateral for loans. In addition, accounts receivable can be sold for immediate cash to factoring companies at a discount of the book value. Given the relative liquidity of working capital, the amount of investment risk is inherently low. An appropriate rate of return to associate with the working capital

Required Return on Intangible Assets & Intellectual Property (IA & IP)

Asset Category	Value ($000s)	Percent	Required Return	Weighted Required Return	Allocated Weighted Return
Net Working Capital	10,000	10%	7.00%	0.70%	7.7%
Fixed Assets	20,000	20%	11.00%	2.20%	2.0%
IA & IP	70,000	70%	13.85%	9.70%	90.3%
INVESTED CAPITAL	100,000	100%		12.60%	100.0%

Exhibit 7.3   Example Company, Inc.

component of the business enterprise is that which is available from investment in short-term securities of low risk levels. The rate available on 90-day certificates of deposit or money market funds serves as an appropriate benchmark.

The tangible or fixed assets of the business are comprised of production machinery, warehouse equipment, transportation fleet, office buildings, office equipment, leasehold improvements, office equipment, and manufacturing plants. The value of this asset category may not be accurately reflected on company balance sheets. Aggressive depreciation policies may state the net book value at an amount lower than the fair market value on which a return should be earned. Correction of this problem can be accomplished by estimating fair market value somewhere in between original equipment costs and net book value. A midpoint between the two points is usually a reasonable compromise. For some industries the original cost can be an appropriate value to use for fixed assets.

An indication of the rate of return that is contributed by these assets can be pegged at about the interest rate at which commercial banks make loans, using the fixed assets as collateral. While these assets are not as liquid as working capital, they can often be sold to other companies. This marketability allows a partial return of the investment in fixed assets should the business fail. Another aspect of relative risk reduction relates to the strategic redeployment of fixed assets. Assets that can be redirected for use elsewhere in a corporation have a degree of versatility, which can still allow an economic contribution to be derived from their employment even if it isn't from the originally intended purpose.

While these assets are more risky than working capital investments, they possess favorable characteristics that must be considered in the weighted average cost of capital allocation. Fixed assets that are very specialized in nature must reflect higher levels of risk, which of course demands a higher rate of return. Specialized assets are those which are not easily redeployed for other commercial exploitation or liquidated to other businesses for other uses. In this example, $20 million is invested in fixed assets.

Intangible assets can be considered to be the most risky asset components of the overall business enterprise. These assets may have little, if any, liquidity and poor versatility for redeployment elsewhere in the business. This enhances their risk. Customized computer software for tracking the results of clinical studies may have very little liquidation value if the company fails. The investment in trained employees that know how to get government approvals may be altogether lost and the value of other elements of a going concern are directly related to the success of the business. A higher rate of return on these assets is therefore required.

An appropriate investment rate of return is then derived and assigned to the intangible assets and intellectual property of the business, including the infringing technology, by using the weighted average cost of capital for the business, the return on fixed assets deemed appropriate, and the return on working capital deemed appropriate. The earnings associated with the intellectual property and intangible assets of the company are then calculated as depicted in Exhibit 7.1. Conversion of these earnings into a royalty rate can be accomplished by dividing the earnings by the associated revenues.

Exhibit 7.3 tells us that over 90 percent of the profits of Example Company, Inc. are derived from intangible assets and intellectual property. If Example Company shows operating profits of 20 percent on sales, then 18 percent of sales (90 percent of the 20 percent profit margin) should be attributed to intangible assets and intellectual property. Depending on the characteristics of the subject technology it may deserve to have the majority of the 18 percent attributed to it for its contribution to the business.

The final allocation requires considering the amount, types, and importance of other intellectual property used in the business. The royalty just derived may include earnings derived by the business from exploitation of intellectual property and intangible assets unrelated to specific technology.

7.4 ROYALTY RATE FOR THE SPECIFIC PATENTED INVENTION OF EXAMPLE COMPANY, INC.

The next step is to answer the following question: How much of a royalty rate should be subtracted from the derived 18 percent royalty rate to isolate the portion that is attributable to only the subject patents? It must be remembered that the 18 percent rate is for all of the intangible assets and intellectual property possessed by Example Company, Inc. including the subject patented invention.

The answer to this question can be estimated by focusing on a company that operates in a similar industry and possesses most of the intellectual property and intangible assets possessed by the infringing company. However, the selected company must be one that does not possess or use the subject proprietary and patented inventions. By

> Investment Rate of Return Associated
> with all Intangible Assets and
> Intellectual Property of
> Example Company, Inc. *Including* the
> Patented Invention in suit.

MINUS

> Investment Rate of Return Associated
> with all Intangible Assets and
> Intellectual Property of
> Surrogate Companies *Excluding* the
> Patented Invention in suit.

EQUALS

> Royalty Rate Associated with the
> Patented Invention suit.

**Exhibit 7.4   Example Company, Inc.
Royalty Rate for Patented Invention in suit**

duplicating the same analysis presented in Exhibit 7.3 for a surrogate company, we can isolate the amount of income to associate with all intangible assets and intellectual property except for the subject patent. When such an analysis is concluded, it is likely that the royalty rate to associate with everything other than the subject patent will be lower. The difference between the rate determined for the company that is not practicing the patent in suit and the 18 percent that was previously determined is the royalty rate to associate with the subject patent. Exhibit 7.4 enumerates this process.

7.5   BENEFITS OF AN INVESTMENT RATE OF RETURN ANALYSIS

An investment rate of return analysis enhances royalty rate determination models by:

- Considering the investment risk associated with the business and industry environment in which the licensed technology will be used.
- Reflecting specific commercialization factors associated with the licensed technology as embedded in forecasts associated with sales, production costs, and operating expenses.
- Allowing for an investment return to be earned on the fixed assets used in the business.
- Allowing for an investment return to be earned on the working capital assets used in the business.
- Allowing for an investment return to be earned on the other intangible assets and intellectual property used in the business *other than* the subject patent.

Use of this method can be limited by the information that is available. Balance sheet information for the business unit that produces the infringing product or service is important to have. Without such information, this method can be difficult to implement.

7.6 SUMMARY

The investment rate of return analysis determines a royalty rate within the context of the business enterprise framework. This method incorporates the value and relative risk of other asset categories used in the business.

8

Discounted
Cash Flow Analysis

A variation of the investment rate of return analysis can be used for royalty rate derivation. This method makes use of a discounted cash flow analysis that converts a stream of expected cash flows into a present value. The conversion of expected cash flows is accomplished by using a discount rate reflecting the risk of the expected cash flows. In addition to the benefits associated with using an investment rate of return analysis, the discounted cash flow analysis also reflects the:

- Time period during which economic benefits will be obtained
- Timing of capital expenditure investments
- Timing of working capital investments
- Timing and amount of other investments in intellectual property and intangible assets not associated with the subject technology

The basis of all value is cash. The net amount of cash flow thrown off by a business is central to corporate value. Net cash flow—also called free cash flow—is the amount of cash remaining after reinvestment in the business to sustain continued viability of the business. Net cash flow can be used for dividends, charity contributions, or diversification investments. Net cash flow is not needed to continue fueling the business. Aggregation of all future net cash flows derived from operating the business, modified with respect to the time value of money, represents the value of a business.

A basic net cash flow calculation is depicted below:

NET SALES minus
MANUFACTURING COSTS equals   (Eq. 8.1)
GROSS PROFITS

GROSS PROFITS minus
RESEARCH EXPENSES and
MARKETING EXPENSES and
GENERAL OVERHEAD EXPENSES and
ADMINISTRATION EXPENSES and
SELLING EXPENSES equal
OPERATING PROFITS

OPERATING PROFITS minus
INCOME TAXES equals
NET INCOME

NET INCOME plus
DEPRECIATION equals
GROSS CASH FLOW

GROSS CASH FLOW minus
ADDITIONS TO WORKING CAPITAL and
ADDITIONS TO FIXED PLANT INVESTMENT equals
NET CASH FLOW

Sales represent the revenue dollars collected by the company from providing products or services to customers. Net sales are the amount of revenues that remain after discounts, returns, and refunds.

Manufacturing costs are the primary costs associated with making or providing the product or service. Included in this expense category are expenses associated with labor, raw materials, manufacturing plant costs, and all other expenses directly related to transforming raw materials into finished goods.

Gross profit is the difference between net sales and manufacturing costs. The level of gross profits reflects manufacturing efficiencies and a general level of product profitability. It does not, however, reflect the ultimate commercial success of a product or service. Many other expenses important to commercial success are not accounted for at the gross profit level. Other expenses contributing to successful commercialization of a product include:

- Research expenses associated with creating new products and enhancing old ones.
- Marketing expenses required for motivating customers to purchase the products or service.
- General overhead expenses required to provide basic corporate support for commercialization activities.
- Selling expenses associated with salaries, commissions, and other activities that keep the product moving into the hands of customers.

Operating profits reflect the amount left over after nonmanufacturing expenses are subtracted from gross profits.

Income taxes are expenses of doing business and must be accounted for in valuing any business initiative.

The depreciation expense is calculated based on the remaining useful life of equipment that is purchased for business purposes. It is a noncash expense that allocates the original amount invested in fixed assets. Depreciation is calculated to account for the deterioration of fixed assets as they are used to produce, market, sell, deliver, and administer the process of generating sales. Depreciation accounts for the "using up" of assets. It is called a noncash expense because the cash associated with the expense was disbursed long ago at the time that fixed assets were purchased and installed. The depreciation expense is subtracted before reaching operating profit so that income taxes will reflect depreciation as an expense of doing business.

Gross cash flow is calculated by adding the depreciation expense, previously subtracted to calculated operating income, back to the after-tax income of the company. Gross cash flow represents the total amount of cash that the business generates each year.

Additions to working capital and additions to fixed plant investment are investments in the business required to fuel continued production capabilities.

Net cash flow is everything that remains of gross cash flow after accounting for reinvestment into the business for fixed plant and working capital additions.

Value is derived from the net cash flows by converting the expected amounts into a present value using discount rates that reflect investment risk and time value of money as previously discussed in Chapter 7.

Note that interest expenses are not part of this analysis. In considering the value of intellectual property, and the royalty rate that should be associated with it, the means by which it is financed has nothing to do with its value. This model is looking to capture the cash flows that the intellectual property can generate from the market place. A debt burden should not be part of such an analysis. If you think of a new car, the price of the car (its value) is the same regardless of how the buyer will finance it. Another example is income-producing real estate. The value of the property is based on the net rental income that the property generates before financing costs. Think of a highly leveraged property. If a property is leveraged to such an extent that no net income is produced because of high interest expenses, it does not mean that the property has zero value. The property might actually be generating fabulous cash flow that is absorbed by a poor financial structure.

In damages analysis we are looking to identify the amount of economic benefit that the infringer wrongly took. As such, the damages analysis should calculate such benefits free of interest expenses. The fact that an infringer used the wrongly taken economic benefits for interest expenses should not excuse the infringer from compensating the infringed. When someone steals a car for a joy ride but claims that they did not have any fun while driving the car they should not be excused from paying restitution.

8.1 PHARMAPROD COMMODITY CORP. VALUE

Consider the discounted cash flow analysis presented in Exhibit 8.1 as a simple example of using discounted cash flow analysis for royalty rate derivation. Exhibit 8.1 represents the future net cash flows for PharmaProd Commodity Corp. as it currently operates. The sales, expenses, and earnings for the company reflect the commodity-like nature of the business. Product prices are under pressure from strong competition translating into low profitability. Strong competition also severely limits the opportunity for the company to achieve any substantial growth in the future. The present value calculation contained in Exhibit 8.1 shows a value for the company at $10,118,000 using a discount rate of 13 percent. The calculation of the value of the company includes the present value of the net cash flows expected after year eleven. Constant growth, reflecting inflation, and minimal volume growth into perpetuity is captured in the final year discount rate factor used in year eleven. The $10.1 million value equals the aggregate value of all the assets of the company. This amount indicates that the company has earned its required weighted average cost of capital and an excess present value of $10,118,000.

PharmaProd Commodity Corp. is planning to embark on a major business initiative with the introduction of a new product using new technology and thus changing itself into New PharmaProd Corp. It will continue to offer its commodity product but also add a new proprietary product to its offerings. The technology will be licensed from another company. Exhibit 8.2 represents the present value of the company including the net cash flows from the existing operations of the company and the net cash flows from the new product initiative. Additional sales, manufacturing costs, and expenses are reflected in the analysis. Also, the additions to working capital and fixed assets required for the new product commercialization effort are reflected. Also reflected in the analysis are the research and development expenses needed to prove

YEAR	1	2	3	4	5	6	7	8	9	10
Sales	25,000	25,750	26,523	27,318	28,138	28,982	29,851	30,747	31,669	32,619
Cost of Sales	12,500	12,875	13,261	13,659	14,069	14,491	14,926	15,373	15,835	16,310
Gross Profit	12,500	12,875	13,261	13,659	14,069	14,491	14,926	15,373	15,835	16,310
Gross Profit Margin	50.0%	50.0%	50.0%	50.0%	50.0%	50.0%	50.0%	50.0%	50.0%	50.0%
Operating Expenses:										
General & Administrative	3,000	3,090	3,183	3,278	3,377	3,478	3,582	3,690	3,800	3,914
Research & Development	0	0	0	0	0	0	0	0	0	0
Marketing	2,500	2,575	2,652	2,732	2,814	2,898	2,985	3,075	3,167	3,262
Selling	5,000	5,150	5,305	5,464	5,628	5,796	5,970	6,149	6,334	6,524
Operating Profit	2,000	2,060	2,122	2,185	2,251	2,319	2,388	2,460	2,534	2,610
Operating Profit Margin	8.0%	8.0%	8.0%	8.0%	8.0%	8.0%	8.0%	8.0%	8.0%	8.0%
Income Taxes	760	783	806	830	855	881	907	935	963	992
Net Income	1,240	1,277	1,316	1,355	1,396	1,437	1,481	1,525	1,571	1,618
Net Profit Margin	5.0%	5.0%	5.0%	5.0%	5.0%	5.0%	5.0%	5.0%	5.0%	5.0%
Cash Flow Calculation:										
+ Depreciation	19	38	59	79	101	123	146	169	193	218
– Working Capital Additions	140	150	155	159	164	169	174	179	184	190
– Capital Expenditures	175	188	193	199	205	211	217	224	231	238
Net Cash Flow	944	978	1,026	1,076	1,128	1,181	1,235	1,291	1,349	1,408
Discount Factor 13%	0.9413	0.8330	0.7372	0.6524	0.5773	0.5109	0.4521	0.4001	0.3541	2.9459
Present Value	888	815	757	702	651	603	558	517	478	4,149
Net Present Value	*10,118*									

Exhibit 8.1 PharmaProd Commodity Corp. Business Enterprise Value

YEAR	1	2	3	4	5	6	7	8	9	10
Sales	25,000	25,750	26,523	27,318	28,138	28,982	29,851	30,747	31,669	32,619
Cost of Sales	12,500	12,875	13,261	13,659	14,069	14,491	14,926	15,373	15,835	16,310
New Product Sales	100	1,000	4,000	8,000	10,000	11,000	12,100	13,310	14,641	15,080
New Product Cost of Sales	35	350	1,400	2,800	3,500	3,850	4,235	4,658.5	5,124	5,278
Gross Profit	12,565	13,525	15,861	18,859	20,569	21,641	22,791	24,025	25,351	26,112
Gross Profit Margin	50.1%	50.6%	52.0%	53.4%	53.9%	54.1%	54.3%	54.5%	54.7%	54.7%
Operating Expenses:										
General & Administrative	3,012	3,210	3,663	4,238	4,577	4,798	5,034	5,287	5,557	5,724
Research & Development	5,000	1,500	0	0	0	0	0	0	0	0
Marketing	2,510	2,675	3,052	3,532	3,814	3,998	4,195	4,406	4,631	4,770
Selling	5,020	5,350	6,105	7,064	7,628	7,996	8,390	8,811	9,262	9,540
Operating Profit	(2,977)	790	3,042	4,025	4,551	4,849	5,171	5,521	5,901	6,078
Operating Profit Margin	-11.6%	3.1%	11.5%	14.7%	16.2%	16.7%	17.3%	18.0%	18.6%	18.6%
Income Taxes	(1,131)	300	1,156	1,530	1,729	1,842	1,965	2,098	2,242	2,310
Net Income	(1,846)	490	1,886	2,496	2,822	3,006	3,206	3,423	3,659	3,768
Net Profit Margin	-7.4%	1.9%	7.1%	9.1%	10.0%	10.4%	10.7%	11.1%	11.6%	11.6%
Cash Flow Calculation:										
+ Depreciation	368	387	408	428	450	472	495	518	542	567
− Working Capital Additions	160	330	755	959	564	369	394	421	451	278
− Capital Expenditures	3,665	188	193	199	205	211	217	224	231	238
Net Cash Flow	(5,303)	360	1,346	1,766	2,503	2,898	3,090	3,296	3,520	3,820
Discount Factor 13%	0.9413	0.833	0.737	0.652	0.5773	0.5109	0.4521	0.4001	0.3541	0.2959
Present Value	(4,992)	300	992	1,152	1,445	1,481	1,397	1,319	1,246	11,253
Net Present Value	*15,593*									

Exhibit 8.2 New PharmaProd Corp. Business Enterprise Value with Licensed Technology

the technology and obtain FDA approvals.[1] As a result of the new business initiative the present value of the company increases to $15,593,000.[2] The higher value reflects the added revenues and earnings of the new product at the higher profit margins of the new product. A comparison of Exhibits 8.1 and 8.2 shows that research, marketing, working capital additions, and fixed asset additions are all higher and by more than just a proportional share of the higher sales forecasts. This is especially true for the early years in the discounted cash flow analysis because the new product initially does not contribute significant sales volume but definitely has expenses.

8.2 NEW PHARMAPROD CORP. ROYALTY RATE

What royalty rate should the company pay for use of the new product technology? The highest amount of royalty the company should be willing to pay for the licensed technology is shown on Exhibit 8.3. A royalty of 10.9 percent of the sales associated with the new product represents a royalty expense to New PharmaProd Corp. and yields a present value of $10,118,000—the initial value of the company. At this royalty rate, the company has earned a return on the additional investment required to commercialize the new product technology and not a penny more. A royalty rate of less than 10.9 percent would increase the value of the company by allowing New PharmaProd Corp. to keep a portion of the excess cash flow generated by the licensed intellectual property.

Note that a payment greater than a 10.9 percent royalty rate would cause the value of the company to drop below the initial $10,118,000.

---

[1] The time span for many pharmaceutical projects is greater than depicted in this example. For illustrative purposes a short time span has been used.

[2] For simplicity the same discount rate of 13 percent has been used. The introduction of the new product initiative might warrant increasing the discount rate as the risk of the company is increased with the introduction of a new product.

YEAR		1	2	3	4	5	6	7	8	9	10
Sales		25,000	25,750	26,523	27,318	28,138	28,982	29,851	30,747	31,669	32,619
Cost of Sales		12,500	12,875	13,261	13,659	14,069	14,491	14,926	15,373	15,835	16,310
New Product Sales		100	1,000	4,000	8,000	10,000	11,000	12,100	13,310	14,641	15,080
New Product Cost of Sales		35	350	1,400	2,800	3,500	3,850	4,235	4,658.5	5,124	5,278
Gross Profit		12,565	13,525	15,861	18,859	20,569	21,641	22,791	24,025	25,351	26,112
Gross Profit Margin		50.1%	50.6%	52.0%	53.4%	53.9%	54.1%	54.3%	54.5%	54.7%	54.7%
Operating Expenses:											
Royalty	10.9%	11	109	437	873	1,092	1,201	1,321	1,453	1,598	1,646
General & Administrative		3,012	3,210	3,663	4,238	4,577	4,798	5,034	5,287	5,557	5,724
Research & Development		5,000	1,500	0	0	0	0	0	0	0	0
Marketing		2,510	2,675	3,052	3,532	3,814	3,998	4,195	4,406	4,631	4,770
Selling		5,020	5,350	6,105	7,064	7,628	7,996	8,390	8,811	9,262	9,540
Operating Profit		(2,988)	681	2,605	3,152	3,460	3,648	3,850	4,068	4,303	4,432
Operating Profit Margin		-12.0%	2.6%	9.8%	11.5%	12.3%	12.6%	12.9%	13.2%	13.6%	13.6%
Income Taxes		(1,135)	259	990	1,198	1,315	1,386	1,463	1,546	1,635	1,684
Net Income		(1,853)	422	1,615	1,954	2,145	2,262	2,387	2,522	2,668	2,748
Net Profit Margin		-7.4%	1.6%	6.1%	7.2%	7.6%	7.8%	8.0%	8.2%	8.4%	8.4%
Cash Flow Calculation:											
+ Depreciation		368	387	408	428	450	472	495	518	542	567
− Working Capital Additions		160	330	755	959	564	369	394	421	451	278
− Capital Expenditures		3,665	188	193	199	205	211	217	224	231	238
Net Cash Flow		(5,310)	292	1,075	1,225	1,826	2,154	2,271	2,396	2,529	2,799
Discount Factor	13%	0.9413	0.833	0.7372	0.6524	0.5773	0.5109	0.4521	0.4001	0.3541	2.9459
Present Value		(4,998)	243	793	799	1,054	1,100	1,027	958	895	8,247
Net Present Value		*10,118*									

Exhibit 8.3   New PharmaProd Corp. Business Enterprise Value with Licensed Technology and a Royalty Payment

In such a case, the company would be in a worse value condition than if it had never instituted the new business initiative.

8.3 LOST VALUE

A discounted cash flow analysis can be used to calculate damages where value has been forever lost. As an example, consider a patent attorney malpractice case where a plaintiff is suing an attorney for missing an important filing date and forever losing a chance to obtain patents in Europe. The amount of damages can be estimated from analyses similar to those presented in Exhibits 8.1 and 8.2. The first discounted cash flow analysis would derive a value for the business assuming the European patents had been properly attained. The second analysis would derive a value using the scenario that European patents did not exist and as a result the second analysis would show lower cash flows and value. The difference in value is the damages caused by the patent attorney.

"Before and after" cash flow projections can be difficult to construct. In some cases, there might not be any hope of developing a European business without the patents that were lost. In such cases the value indicated by the differential calculation will be significant. In other circumstances a small diminution in European cash flows due to the lost patent protection may be all that results and causes a small loss in value.

8.4 SUMMARY

Considering the importance of intellectual property, a comprehensive analysis that reflects revenues, profits, expenses, and investment is justified to isolate the income attributed to intellectual property and to form the basis for royalty rate negotiations.

9

Market-Derived Royalty Rates

Indications of reasonable royalties can sometimes be derived from market transactions but care is required. The amount at which independent parties licensed similar intellectual property can provide an indication for a reasonable royalty. In fact, a large part of establishing infringement damage has been testimony presented by experts. These experts cite the royalty rates contained in licenses of similar intellectual property that were negotiated between unrelated parties and, relying on these precedents, conclude a proxy royalty rate for calculating infringement damages.

Market transactions considered useful for deriving reasonable royalties are usually between unrelated parties where intellectual property is the focal point of the deal. When a market transaction centers on intellectual property similar to the infringed property, the royalty terms of the transaction may be appropriate for application to the infringed property. Transactions most often cited as useful indications for reasonable royalties are license agreements which disclose the compensation terms for similar property.

Suppose that a personal shaving product has been enhanced by a safety feature that prevents the blades from ever nicking or cutting the consumer's face or legs. Suppose that the feature is patented, valid, and infringed. A reasonable royalty for use in fixing damages might be determined by looking at the amount of royalty paid by other shaving manufacturers for similar safety features. Unfortunately, such agreements are nearly impossible to discover. Very often license agreements involving similar intellectual property just do not exist. When such agreements are actually discovered, there isn't any guarantee that the parties involved will be eager to disclose specific details that would be useful for comparative purposes. Even if all of the specific details of a comparable transaction can be discovered, many hurdles remain before the market transaction can be considered as a reliable indication of a reasonable royalty for application to a specific infringement case.

Many aspects of market transactions should be studied before a specific transaction can be concluded as representing a reasonable royalty for use in a specific infringement case. The remainder of this chapter considers the appropriateness of using the royalty terms of similar licenses as a proxy for infringement damages when analyzing similar intellectual property licenses.

9.1 INTERNAL LICENSES ARE OFTEN SELF-SERVING

Multinational corporations often transfer intellectual property to foreign subsidiaries. Parent companies often own keystone intellectual property and their subsidiaries hold licenses allowing them to use the property. These licenses are referred to as internal licenses. Many of the royalty terms in these types of transactions are structured to shift income into jurisdictions with lower income tax burdens. Hence, the royalty rate may not reflect the economic contribution of the intellectual property. Instead it may be more reflective of differential corporate income tax rates between a multi-national corporate parent and a foreign subsidiary. Various tax authorities in many countries, including the United States, are clearing the cloud hanging over these international transfers. Tax specialists around the world are diligently looking at internal licenses for the reasonableness of royalty rates. As such, the royalty rates between international related parties are becoming more arms-length.

9.2 RELEVANT TIME PERIOD

When analyzing stock purchases, investors don't give much consideration to the price paid for stocks 20 years, 10 years, 5 years, or even a year ago. Considerations that are fundamental to pricing common stock include earnings growth prospects, expectations for economic growth, competitor analysis, inflation trends, and a myriad of other expectations about the future, all of which affect future cash flows to investors. The future is the focal point. Expected cash flows determine the amount that investors will pay for a stock. The price paid for a stock in the past is an interesting notation but has little to do with a current pricing analysis. The same is true when corporations engage in mergers and acquisitions. The prices at which businesses are exchanged seldom relate to amounts at which prior transactions were consummated.

When considering the purchase of an investment real estate property, a lot of analysis goes into determining the price to offer. Included are consideration of prevailing interest rates, inflation, rental income, operating expenses, property taxes, and income taxes. All of these considerations are analyzed from the perspective of quantifying future expectations about profits and return on investment. Very little, if any, consideration is given to the price at which the property has historically changed hands. Manhattan Island was purchased from the original owners for $24 worth of novelty trinkets. Historic transaction prices are interesting footnotes but not usually relevant for current transaction pricing.

It is no different for intellectual property. A reasonable royalty must be based on future expectations that both the licensee and the licenser individually possess and which eventually converge as negotiations reach a conclusion. Reasonable royalties must be determined with an eye to the future. The amount paid years ago for licensing intellectual property may not be relevant in light of changing industry conditions.

When considering *aged* royalty rates as a proxy for damages, also consider the fundamental industry, economic, and cultural changes that have occurred since the signing of the comparable license and how the past conditions compare with those in the present.

9.3   FINANCIAL CONDITION OF BOTH LICENSING PARTIES

When one of the parties in a similar license is desperate to complete the transaction, the amount paid for the license is clouded. A nearly bankrupt licenser may not have enough time to shop for the best offer and could leave a significant amount of money on the negotiating table. On the other hand, a manufacturing company with obsolete technology may find itself going out of business without access to new technology. This my force them to agree to extraordinary terms, at least temporarily.

A fair and reasonable royalty is best determined in an environment where both of the negotiating parties are on equal footing. Both parties should have the option to walk away from the deal. When ancillary forces are compelling one of the negotiating parties to capitulate to the demands of the other then a fair and reasonable royalty may be not indicated in such a license agreement. An important question to consider is—"Were both parties on equal footing when the proxy royalty rate was negotiated?"

9.4   RELEVANT INDUSTRY TRANSACTIONS

Some licenses may involve property that is similar to the infringed property but the property is licensed for use in a different industry. To be useful for infringement damages a proxy royalty rate must have been negotiated for similar property that is used in a similar industry.

Each industry has its own set of unique economic forces. Some, such as consumer electronics, are highly competitive. Others, like airlines, are oligopolies. Some industries are sensitive to interest rates (construction). Others are not (food). Some industries are under strong pressure from foreign producers (apparel). Others are only regionally competitive (gravel quarries). All of these factors drive the profitability and growth prospects of the industry participants. These factors also impact the amount of economic benefits that intellectual property can contribute to a commercial operation, which directly relates to the royalties that can be considered reasonable.

A world class trademark could contribute as much as, or even more than, 30 percent of sales as direct economic benefits when used in its core industry. Coca-Cola might be an example of a trademark that could possibly command a double-digit royalty if it were licensed for use in the soft drink industry. However, the use of the Coca-Cola trademark on sports clothing couldn't possibly command such a royalty. The vast amount of competition for sports clothing and the low profit margins in the apparel industry would drive the royalty downward into single digits. A royalty from a deal that licensed the Coca-Cola trademark into the apparel industry would be useless as a proxy for an appropriate royalty to use in licensing the same trademark in the soft drink industry. Licenses should be carefully analyzed for industry relevance.

(a) International Transactions

In developing nations where intellectual property protection is weak the amount paid for a license would likely be far less than in developed nations where intellectual property rights are protected and respected. This assumes that an intellectual property owner would even consider allowing for the use of its property in such countries. A low rate in developing nations reflects the fact that protection of the property may not be realistic regardless of what the license agreement says.

Economic factors in many countries are also different, so the royalties that can be supported in various countries differs. As such, license agreements in different countries might possess different royalty rates for the same intellectual property, none of which may be relevant for infringement damages calculations. Foreign licenses must be compared to countries with comparable economic prosperity to be useful for infringement damages.

(b) Intellectual Property Remaining Life

The discussion in Chapter 5, under Georgia-Pacific, Factor 7 also is pertinent here. Overall, the term of the license is not always related to the level of the royalty rate.

(c) Complementary Asset Investment Requirements

Regardless of remaining economic life, a significant investment in complementary assets will affect the royalty negotiation. Intellectual property that is associated with a product that delivers a 40 percent operating profit is a wonderful property indeed. A very high royalty might be warranted. But if this same intellectual property requires a billion dollar up-front investment, royalty amounts may not be as stellar.

(d) Non-monetary Compensation

Compensation for the use of intellectual property can take many different forms. Sometimes cash alone is the basis of licensing compensation—a cash payment is made by the licensee and no further payments are required. Lump sum payments with additional running royalties are another example of license compensation. Running royalties alone are another example. Sometimes the licenser gets a royalty and also an equity interest in the licensee's company. Sometimes the licenser gets only an equity interest. License agreements can also call for the licensee to share technological enhancements, as grant-backs, with the licenser. In return, the licensee might demand a lower royalty rate because a portion of the licenser's compensation will be in the form of access to enhancements of the original property.

For infringement damages a reasonable royalty is usually specified as a running royalty with no other forms of compensation. For similar license agreements to be used as a proxy for damages, the form of license compensation must be on a like-kind basis. A trademark license might call for an up-front payment of $1 million plus a running royalty of 5 percent of sales. The up-front payment might represent several percentage points of running royalty in some circumstances. Without an up-front payment the license might have called for a running royalty of 6 percent, instead of 5 percent. In deriving a reasonable royalty rate for damages, the entire compensation package of a similar license must be translated to an amount that presents a running royalty as the sole form of license compensation. This conversion can be very difficult when licenses call for cross-licensing of technology. The problem then becomes determining the value of the technology exchanged and representation of the value as a running royalty rate. Proxy licenses must be looked at for like-kind compensation.

(e) Exclusivity

What should the basis of reasonable royalties be regarding the aspect of exclusivity? Typically, higher royalty rates are associated with license agreements providing the licensee with exclusive rights to use the intellectual property. Exclusive rights to use a keystone intellectual property place the licensee in a superior position. If the intellectual property provides highly desirable utility then premium prices can be demanded for the product. Competitors cannot counter with the same product without risking infringement, and the exclusive licensee will earn superior profits. Such an arrangement is worth higher royalty payments. DuPont renegotiated a license involving worldwide and exclusive rights to a drug patent. They changed the agreement to a non-exclusive basis. As a result the royalty dropped from 5.5 percent of sales for exclusive rights to 4 percent of sales for non-exclusive rights.

9.5 GOVERNMENTAL REGULATIONS

Foreign licenses and their royalty rates may be inappropriate for use as a basis for a damages royalty. Foreign governments sometimes intervene in the amount of royalty that can be charged to technology transfers. Government established royalties very often have little to do with the economic contribution of intellectual property. The royalties are more likely the result of international trade and taxation policies. Foreign governments may also require that a certain portion of product manufacturing be conducted in host countries. Final assembly may be all that is required, or perhaps significant portions of fundamental manufacturing must be done in the host country. Labor laws may be more restrictive. Many of the regulations could be different from those of the country in which infringement took place. These regulations will affect the profitability of the foreign licensee and impact the amount that is available for royalty payments. Political instability could make privatization a real possibility and, along with the loss of a private business, the licensed technology could also be expropriated. All of these foreign government characteristics affect the profitability that can be attained with licensed property and the risk of the licensee's investment. All of these conditions affect the royalty. As such, a royalty associated with a foreign licensing transaction may not be appropriate for use in establishing a reasonable royalty for a domestic transaction.

9.6 ARE THE INDEPENDENT PARTIES REALLY INDEPENDENT?

Independent parties that negotiate a license for intellectual property similar to the infringed property are not always as independent as they seem. Even when the two companies are separate corporations, the royalty rate that is being considered as a proxy for infringement damages may be clouded.

Strategic alliances are becoming more prevalent. Corporations are realizing that they cannot independently become masters of the many different and complex technologies that they need. Many corporations are involved in joint ventures, licenses, distribution agreements, services agreements, and other arrangements that make them into partners, at least on a limited basis. It is common for corporations to have a number of alliances with different corporations. Merck & Co. is involved with different joint ventures which include separate partnerships with Johnson & Johnson and DuPont. Also becoming common are corporations that have several different alliances with the same company.

When one independent company has several alliances with another independent company are they still really negotiating at arm's length? One specific license agreement may not be independent of others that also exist between the two parties. One specific license agreement, containing a royalty rate that is being considered as a proxy for infringement damages, may have been negotiated as part of a package of license agreements. The negotiated royalty may have been a trade-off for other points of negotiation in other areas of their relationship. A favorable royalty may have been granted to one of the parties in exchange for a trade-off regarding a completely different strategic alliance in which the same parties participate. Licenses that are to serve as similar transactions for establishing infringement damages are most useful when truly independent parties negotiated in their own self interests.

9.7   OUTCOME OF AN INFRINGEMENT LAWSUIT

Licenses to be used as a proxy for infringement damages may arise from the outcome of an unrelated infringement lawsuit. The infringer may find itself permanently enjoined from using the intellectual property. Looking around for alternative intellectual property, the infringer may find that the intellectual property it is barred from using is the best alternative. If the plaintiff is willing, a license deal may be struck allowing the infringer to once again use the intellectual property. This type of proxy for infringement damages may be some of the best market evidence available for establishing infringement damages. Such an agreement could safely be assumed to have been negotiated between two parties negotiating in their own self interests with both being fully aware of all relevant facts, including alternative intellectual property (as was probably brought out in great detail during the infringement trial). The infringer, now turned would-be licensee, could walk away from a license deal, but instead negotiates a license for the intellectual property.

9.8 SUMMARY

Establishing reasonable royalties for calculating infringement damages is often accomplished by looking at the royalty terms specified in licenses involving similar intellectual property. Many aspects of the license agreement must be analyzed for the royalty provision to be a useful proxy.

10

Royalty Rate
Rules of Thumb

S ome of the more commonly used royalty rate development methods are discussed in this chapter. They are attractive because of their simplicity—they are easy to understand and use. The methods are popular because of their universal application. In some cases they can provide a reasonable indication of the range into which the final answer should fall. Keep in mind, however, that it is not usually a good idea to rely solely on rules of thumb for deriving a royalty rate.

The difficulty with rules of thumb is that they do not reflect many of the most important factors that are part of commercializing intellectual property. The profits that are derived from commercialization of intellectual property are high on the list of important factors to consider in deriving a royalty rate. Royalties usually relate to profits. Capital expenditures and investments in other intangible assets have also played an important role in some of the models that have been demonstrated elsewhere in this book. Higher amounts of investment often translate to downward pressure on the level of royalty that can be paid. Business risk has also been shown to affect the amount of royalty that can be paid. When investment risk is high, royalty levels are pressured downward. The caveat with most of the rules of thumb in this chapter is a lack of direct consideration for these important factors.

10.1   THE 25 PERCENT RULE

Fully stated, this method calculates a royalty as 25 percent to 33⅓ percent of the gross profit, before taxes, from the enterprise operations in which the licensed intellectual property is used. Gross profit has never been accurately defined where this rule is discussed. Gross profits, based on generally accepted accounting principles, reflect the direct costs of production—manufacturing expenses. These include raw material costs, direct labor costs, utility expenses, and even the depreciation expenses of the manufacturing facilities. All of the costs and expenses associated with conversion of raw materials into a final product or service are captured in the gross profit figure. Since this is often the area of greatest contribution from intellectual property, consideration of the amount of gross profits is reasonable. It fails, however, to consider the final profitability that is ultimately realized from the intellectual property. Absent from the analysis are operating expenses such as selling, administrative, and general overhead expenses. An argument for eliminating operating expenses from the analysis might center on the idea that the value of intellectual property, such as manufacturing technology, is best measured by the enhancement of profits in the area of the business in which they have the most direct effect. However, a more broadened view however shows that an intellectual property royalty can be affected by selling expenses and other ongoing operating expenses that are part of the commercialization.

Intellectual property that is part of a product or service which requires small amounts of marketing, advertising, and selling effort is far more valuable than a product based upon intellectual property that requires huge efforts in these areas. When national advertising campaigns, highly compensated sales personnel, and highly skilled technical support people are needed to provide customer support, bottom line profits are lowered.

Two patented products may cost the same amount to produce and yield the same amount of gross profit. Yet, one of the products may require extensive and continuing sales support. The added costs of these sales efforts make this product less profitable to the licensee. While the two products may have the same gross profit margins, it is very unlikely that they would command the same royalty, given the different assumptions about selling and support costs.

The operating profit level, after consideration of the nonmanufacturing operating expenses, is a far more accurate determinant of the contribution of the intellectual property. The royalty for specific intellectual property must reflect the industry and economic environment in which the property is used. Some environments are competitive and require a lot of support costs which reduce net profits. Intellectual property that is used in this type of environment is not as valuable as intellectual property in a high-profit environment where lower support costs are required. A proper royalty must reflect this aspect of the economic environment. A royalty based on gross profits alone cannot reflect this reality. The rule is better when applied to operating profit margins.

The percentage of gross profit that should ultimately go to the licenser is considered by most advocates of the 25 Percent Rule to be flexible. Yet when a licensee must heavily invest in complementary assets, a lower percentage of profit may be more proper. If very little investment is needed then a royalty based on a larger share of profits may go to the licenser. Intuitively this is correct, yet the methodology provides no clues as to quantifying a relationship between licensee capital investment and the percentage of gross profit that goes to royalty.

The 25 Percent Rule also fails to consider the other key royalty determinants of risk and fair rates of return on investment. As demonstrated in this book, investment risk is an important factor in determining the value of an investment. This includes the value of intellectual property investments. Higher risk rates generally indicate lower investment values. Lower investment values mean that lower royalty rates are indicated. A royalty method focusing on gross profits does not even begin to capture the risk that is associated with the business in which the intellectual property is used.

Application of this rule of thumb can be narrow-minded. Suppose several patented features that are independent of each other are part of a product. In fact, suppose that five patented features are part of a product and that the operating profit margin after all expenses for making, selling, and managing the product is 20 percent of sales.

Application of the 25 Percent Rule indicates that one of the patented features is worth a 5 percent royalty rate. If the other patented features are also blindly valued using this rule they are each valued at a 5 percent royalty rate. The total royalty rate on the product then becomes 25 percent, which is more than the total operating profit margin.

Too many important factors cannot be reconciled with the 25 Percent Rule. Using this method in negotiating a royalty rate is very difficult. There are many factors to be considered in selecting an appropriate split of profits. Unstructured consideration of these important factors, absent a formalized investment analysis, is bound to omit from consideration too many important considerations. The 25 Percent Rule can be useful as a general guide for deriving an appropriate royalty rate on a limited basis. This rule of thumb is useful in determining an order of magnitude for a royalty rate.

10.2 INDUSTRY NORMS

This royalty rate determination methodology misses even more of the important elements than the 25 Percent Rule. Here, in addition to the other failures of the 25 Percent Rule, consideration of the profitability of the enterprise using the intellectual property is lacking. The Industry Norm method focuses on the rates that others are charging for intellectual property licensed within the same industry. Investment risks, net profits, market size, growth potential, and complementary asset investment requirements are all absent from direct consideration. The use of Industry Norms places total reliance on the ability of others to correctly consider and interpret the many factors affecting royalties. It also places total reliance on the abilities of the founders of the Industry Norm rate. Any mistakes made by the initial setting of an industry royalty are passed along. It is also difficult for many industries to identify a "norm."

10.3 RETURN ON R&D COSTS

When considering a reasonable royalty, the amount spent on development of the intellectual property is a terribly attractive factor to consider. Unfortunately, development costs are also terribly misleading. The main theme of the analysis presented throughout this book concentrates on providing a fair rate of return on the value of the intellectual property assets. The amount spent in the development is rarely equal to the value of the property. A proper royalty should provide a fair return on the value of the asset regardless of the costs incurred in development.

The underlying value of intellectual property is founded on the amount of future economic benefits that are expected to be derived from commercialization of the property. Factors that can limit these benefits include the market potential, the sensitivity of profits to production costs, the period of time over which benefits will be enjoyed, and the many other economic factors previously discussed. The development costs do not reflect these factors in any way, shape, or form. Basing a royalty on development costs can completely miss the goal of obtaining a fair return on a valuable asset.

The U.S. Government spent many millions of dollars on development of nuclear-powered aircraft engines in the 1950s. Engines were tested and prototypes were built. Aircraft were designed and development costs soared. Nuclear-powered aircraft engines were unfortunately never able to deliver the thrust needed to get aircraft airborne. As such, the value of nuclear aircraft engine technology would appropriately be considered low (zero). But, a royalty method based on development costs would indicate a high royalty because future economic benefits are not a factor in the calculation. Whenever someone cites development costs as a reason for a high royalty, remind that person of the royalty they would likely pay for nuclear-powered aircraft engine technology.

10.4   VARIABLE PROFIT SPLIT

Variable profits were previously defined in Chapter 4. Variable profits are the profits earned on an incremental basis after fixed costs are covered. Some experts have suggested that a willing licenser would agree to pay 100 percent of variable profits after fixed costs are covered. Not in a million years would this be a reasonable expectation. Why would a licenser be content to only cover fixed operating costs? Where would the return on the investment in complementary assets—such as the monetary, fixed, and other intangible assets—come from if all of the variable profits were handed away as a royalty payment? Other experts like to apply industry rules of thumb to variable profits. The good news in using this type of royalty rate methodology is that someone has taken the time to calculate the variable profits expected from commercialization of the subject intellectual property. The bad news is that the rule of thumb percentage applied to the variable profits has all of the same weaknesses as the 25 Percent Rule applied to gross profits.

10.5   THE 5 PERCENT OF SALES METHOD

For unknown reasons one of the most popular royalty rates is 5 percent of sales: Sales multiplied by .05 equals the royalty payment. This rate shows up in a lot of different industries. It is associated with embryonic technology and mature trademarks. It has been found in the food, industrial equipment, electronics, construction, and medical device industries. Forget profits, capital investment, earnings growth, operating expenses, investment risk, and even development costs. Somehow 5 percent of sales prevails. Don't be fooled. It's not a magic bullet answer. It does not consider any of the factors discussed in this book and when offered as the correct answer it should be immediately regarded with great suspicion unless suggested by other analyses.

10.6   NEW PRODUCT LICENSING AND ROYALTY RATE CONSIDERATIONS

When someone considers licensing a technology or trademark they usually frame their analysis according to the potential for commercial exploitation of the product. All of the factors listed in this section have an impact on the decision to license and the amount of royalty that a licensee is willing to pay. The factors discussed are far too complex to be captured in simplistic rules of thumb. Most of these factors can however, with relative accuracy, be reflected in the types of investment analysis models presented throughout this book. Important considerations are listed along with the general effect (allowing for interesting exceptions) on royalty rates. A perfect rule of thumb would consider all of the following factors.

Market size and market share.   A large market means more opportunity for successful commercialization. More opportunity will exist for making sales and profits. A larger market potential can represent justification for substantial capital expenditures that might be needed to commercialize intellectual property. If a large market share can be captured, then manufacturing and marketing synergies may ultimately enhance profitability. Royalty rates for intellectual property serving a large market would, in general, be higher than royalties associated with intellectual property used in a product with small market potential. A perfect rule of thumb would also reflect that, in some cases, small and specialized markets allow for extraordinary profit margins where very high royalty rates are also justified.

Performance of existing products.   High royalties are typically associated with high performance products. This is especially true when existing products completely lack product attributes offered by the licensed intellectual property. Superior performance products usually allow for premium pricing, and enhanced profits follow. Intellectual property that provides real product enhancements usually commands higher royalties. "Me-too" products that incorporate marginal performance enhancements generally do not generate superior profits and cannot support significant levels of royalties.

Cannibalization of existing product line. The licensee's expectations of the overall net sales increase that might be enjoyed are an important consideration. When new revenues are derived from new product sales, old product line sales can be simultaneously lowered. Sometimes the new product has only replaced sales dollars and not contributed new revenues. High royalties are not likely for an intellectual property that merely serves as a substitute sale. A high royalty would be expected, however, if the overall effect of the cannibalization brought a net increase in sales and profits. One more possibility involves obsolescence. A licensee using obsolete technology, or a blemished trademark, might be willing to pay a high royalty for cannibalizing new products if it is the only way to stay in business. The new product may replace all sales previously derived from the old product but without the new technology or trademark, no sales may exist at all. When the old product line is obsolete and the only way to stay in business is to license new technology, a high royalty may prevail.

Potential product sales and growth patterns. Faster sales growth usually means obtaining more market share. This leads to higher manufacturing volumes which allows for the development of manufacturing and marketing synergies. Higher profits quickly follow. Fast sales growth allows for initial start-up investments to be quickly recaptured. More earnings are then available to serve as the basis for a return on intellectual property. Fast penetration of a market is highly desirable. Intellectual property that can cause the demand for a new product to accelerate should command a high royalty.

Product life cycle. Short product lives are not good for generating high royalty rates. New products require initial investments in assets.

They require sales personnel and training programs. They divert management energies and cause the company to accept investment risk. When all of these investments must be recaptured and rewarded over the span of a short product life, the risk of failure is exacerbated and high royalties are less likely. When a product is expected to deliver huge sales volumes and vast profits for decades to come, then a high royalty is more likely. A perfect rule of thumb model would also consider that sometimes licensing a technology for a short period is vital for the long-term interests of a company, and in such cases, a high royalty rate might be appropriate.

Investment requirements for commercialization. A technology that is ready to go into full-scale commercialization is more valuable than intellectual property requiring development time and funding. Intellectual property that only requires refinement of manufacturing designs will command a greater royalty over technology that still needs to prove new science. The stage of development is important and applies to trademarks as well. Lower royalties are going to be associated with a trademark requiring huge investments in innovative promotional activities. An already well-recognized trademark commands a much higher royalty.

Investment requirement for manufacturing equipment. A large investment in capital equipment generally diminishes the ability of intellectual property to command a high royalty. A property that requires small equipment investments is generally going to be much more valuable than intellectual property requiring billions of dollars of new equipment.

Investment requirements in complementary intangible assets. Intellectual property cannot deliver economic benefits alone. Other assets are needed in the form of monetary, fixed, and intangible assets. As previously discussed, various types of intangible assets work together for the exploitation of intellectual property. Intangibles such as distribution networks, trademarks, manufacturing procedures, computer software, and others are expensive to create and can be very valuable. Intellectual property requiring a significant investment for development of complementary intangible assets is not going to be able to command a high royalty. When less intangible asset investment is needed to exploit new intellectual property, then higher royalty rates can be expected.

Profit margins. High profits, all other things being equal, drive royalty rates higher. Low profits often can't provide a fair investment return on the value of complementary assets, not to mention the intellectual property that generates the low profits. Low profits, all other things being equal, drive royalties downward. A perfect rule of thumb model would also consider circumstances where low-profit products generate sales of higher profit products. In these cases, a high royalty rate on a low-profit product might be appropriate.

10.7 DESIGN-AROUND COSTS

This rule of thumb has some important relevance for unique infringement cases. In a license negotiation where a new design can circumvent infringement of a patent, the greatest amount of royalty that a licensor would pay is defined by the amount that would be incurred to accomplish the new design. These costs might need to include retooling of the manufacturing facilities and a recall of products in the marketplace. However, if such actions can accomplish the same results as those offered by the patented invention, then the amounts spent for the new design represent the amount of royalty that a reasonable licensor would offer. If the licensor wants more than this amount, a prudent businessperson would most likely make the changes and pass on taking a license. At least two important assumptions are call for:

1. The design-around alternative must accomplish similar utility without infringing the patent that is the subject of negotiations.
2. The design-around effort should not require a significant delay for market entry of the product.

A delay in market entry of a new product can have significant consequences on the investment returns associated with a new product project. Market share that might be gained from rapid entry into the market may be permanently lost or expensive to recapture. When design-around efforts can be accomplished quickly, then the additional product costs associated with escaping the patent serve as a basis for royalty rate determination.

10.8 SUMMARY

Intellectual property that requires a lot of development work is going to command a lower royalty than intellectual property that is fully developed and proven. The other assets that a licensee must commit to the new product also take away from the amount of royalty that a licensee is willing to pay. When a new product is fully developed and the licensee will not need to make a significant initial investment, the situation is ripe for requesting a high royalty rate.

The financial models discussed in this book directly consider most of the important economic factors that drive royalty rates. Royalty rates derived from the financial models are based on sound analysis. Royalty rates derived from rules of thumb are based on rumor and should be supported by additional analyses.

11

Trademark Infringement

by Gordon V. Smith
President
AUS Consultants

E stimating the monetary damages resulting from trademark infringement can be difficult because the circumstances and results of infringement can vary so widely. The infringement of a patent raises binary questions having clear alternatives: Is the patent valid or not? Is the patent embodied in the infringer's product or not? If the patent is valid and firmly ensconced in the infringer's product, then damages are due to the patent owner. Those damages are measured by the owner's lost profits or a reasonable royalty.

The questions in the trademark situation do not point such a clear path to a damage quantification. At one extreme, a counterfeiter simply adopts the verbatim trademark of another and uses it on identically-appearing goods or services. At the other end of the spectrum of possibilities is the infringer's use of a part of a phrase, a color, or some aspect of trade dress—perhaps on a product or service that the mark's owner does not even offer. These examples illustrate one of the practical problems in determining what, if anything, should happen to an infringer as a result of his actions. In some cases, it is most difficult, if not impossible, to quantify the damages of infringement to the mark's rightful owner. Should there then be no recompense to the owner or penalty imposed on the infringer? Irrespective of damages to the owner, the infringer has profited to some degree by usurping the mark and the law and logic would dictate that some or all of those ill-gotten gains be disgorged. Some action also needs to be taken to deter other would-be infringers. Therefore, some action against an infringer is required even if there is no quantifiable damage to the mark's rightful owner.

When the evidence indicates that damage has occurred, it may still be a difficult task to quantify trademark damages because of the fact that there are degrees of damage due to the many and varied ways that one can usurp the identity and goodwill of another. The following examples illustrate some of these ways.

Someone uses a logo similar to ours, or with our color(s), or adopts a few words from our phrase or slogan on a product that is different from ours.

Someone uses an obvious parody of our trademark in a way that we find to be disparaging, derogatory, or degrading.

Someone engages in false advertising that is obviously aimed at our trademark.

A giant corporation usurps (we think) some element of our trademark so that we appear to be infringing on them (reverse confusion).

Someone uses our trademark on shoddy goods that are priced so differently from ours that they are in an entirely separate market.

Someone uses an element of our trademark on their goods or services, with the result that some consumers are confused, to some degree, about the origin of those goods or services.

These examples illustrate the degrees of subjectivity that can exist in evaluating trademark infringement damages, and in quantifying them.

11.1 THE LAW AND MONETARY RELIEF

Trademark infringement disputes are most often resolved by the courts in the of form of injunctive relief. Monetary relief is not an issue in this case.

The courts have considerable latitude in granting monetary relief. The court may award up to three times the amount of otherwise determined damages or profits, according to the facts of the case. Usually, this is done when the infringer acted willfully and with "reckless dis-regard to the trademark owner's rights." As with the award of costs and/or attorney's fees to the prevailing party, this is a matter for the court, and does not relate to the economic support for monetary relief.

As to damages, the Lanham Act tells us:

> When a violation of any right of the registrant of a mark registered in the patent and trademark office, or a violation under section 43(a), shall have been established in any civil action arising under that Act, the plaintiff shall be enti-tled . . . subject to the principles of equity, to recover (1) defendant's profits, (2) any damages sustained by the plain-tiff, and (3) the costs of the action. The court shall assess such profits and damages or cause the same to be assessed under its direction. In assessing profits the plaintiff shall be required to prove defendant's sales only; defendant must prove all elements of cost or deduction claimed. In assess-ing damages the court may enter judgment, according to the circumstance of the case, for any sum above the amount found as actual damages, not exceeding three times such amount. If the court shall find that the amount of the recov-ery based on profits is either inadequate or excessive the court may in its discretion enter judgment for such sum as the court shall find to be just, according to the circum-stances of the case. Such sum in either of the above cir-cumstances shall constitute compensation and not a penalty. The court in exceptional cases may award reasonable attor-ney fees to the prevailing party.[1]

In practice, the courts seem to depend on evidence that (a) the plaintiff has been injured, (b) that the infringer has been unjustly

---

[1] 15 U.S.C. sect. 1117(a).

enriched, or (c) that the infringement has caused confusion in the marketplace relative to the origin of the goods or services in question.

11.2 INFRINGER'S PROFITS

This is perhaps the murkiest area because of the lack of guidance in the law. While it may seem straightforward, the quantification of the infringer's profits may be difficult. To put this task in perspective, let us examine a sample income statement:

Gross Sales	$10,000,000
Less: Returns	50,000
Net Sales	9,950,000
Cost of Goods Sold	6,500,000
Gross Profit	3,450,000
Selling, General, and Administrative Expense	1,250,000
Net Operating Income	2,200,000
Interest Expense	400,000
Other Income (Expense)	(250,000)
Pre-Tax Net Income	1,500,000
Income Taxes	620,000
Net Income	$ 880,000

The law stipulates that the plaintiff needs only to prove the amount of the defendant's sales. The defendant must prove the elements of expense that should be deducted in arriving at "profits." If we start at the bottom of the income statement, we can evaluate the various possible measures of the defendant's profit. Assume, for this purpose, that the income statement reports only the financial results relating to the infringing product or service.

Net income. While this might be presented by the defendant as a proper measure of profits, is it appropriate in the case of infringement? Perhaps not, because expenses of running the infringer's business (including taxes) unrelated to the goods or services in question will be paid by the infringing activity.

Pre-tax net income. This removes the tax issue, but we can observe that this measure of profits is reduced by the amount of interest expense of the defendant as well as by other expenses not specifically related to this product. The profits associated with the alleged infringement should not be influenced by the manner in which the defendant has chosen to capitalize its business, or by unrelated income or expenses.

Net operating income. This is closer to a reasonable measure, but this level of income is affected by the magnitude of selling, general, and administrative expenses. These are highly variable and could, as an example, be quite high if the alleged infringer was breaking into a new market with the infringing mark. That would, at the least, reduce this measure of damages and could even eliminate it. It is not unusual to have no or negative net operating income in the circumstance of market penetration. Should the damages be zero in that case? Obviously not.

Gross profit. From an accounting and economic perspective, measuring damages at this level probably makes the most sense in most cases. It is unlikely that someone would enter into a business in which the gross profit was marginal or negative. That could be the case with a new product if there was a very "steep" learning curve associated with its production, or if there were great economies of scale in the production process that had to be achieved over time, but it would not be very common.

11.3 CONSIDERATIONS IN QUANTIFYING PROFITS

It would be ideal if we could start with an income statement based on the sales of the infringing goods or services. Because this is unlikely to be available in real life, we are faced with the task of creating such an income statement (or at least the parts of it that we deem relevant) from the information that is available.

(a) The Income Statement Elements

Isolating the relevant income streams.   In the previous sample income statement, we assume that we have available a stand-alone income statement for the infringing product or service. That is not typical. Small companies are not likely to have accounting systems in place to permit such a segregation. Large corporations are likely to have financials by product line, but these will contain many allocations of expense that cloud the determination of profits by product or service. The infringing item may have had only limited geographical or retailer distribution. This requires further subdivision of the data.

Expense allocations.   In a business with several products, divisions, or lines of business, many expenses such as those associated with treasury, legal, accounting, research, or corporate advertising functions are not incurred on a product-line basis and must be allocated to each product according to some formula. A formula may be based on sales revenue, number of employees, square footage of production facilities, capital employed, accounts receivable, or any combination of these. Expense allocations in a large organization may be made more complex by being multi-level. Some expenses may be allocated among several products within a product line. At the same time, other expenses are allocated to a product based on its place in a division, subsidiary, or business segment. Expenses may be allocated based on legal entities that are quite different from operating groups.

Our approach is generally to reduce these allocations to their "lowest common denominator" so that we can reassemble them selectively, using those we find appropriate and discarding the others.

One-time or out-of-period events. Costs resulting from one-time or unusual events must also be considered. For example, if a plant is closed the costs of closing as well as ongoing expenses associated with the discontinued operation may be allocated to the surviving operations. This would not be an appropriate expense to reflect in a determination of an infringer's profits. A casualty loss or accounting adjustment would be other examples. One must also be sensitive to adjustments made for events that took place before the period of infringement.

Accounting issues. Another conceptual issue that must be addressed is whether expenses should be based on incremental or fully-absorbed costs. Financial statements are typically expressed on the basis of fully-absorbed costs. Simply stated, this means that each accounting entity, whether a product, product line, division, or segment, must bear its share of allocable expenses. There have been many debates as to whether infringer's profits should be measured on an incremental or fully-absorbed basis. These accounting complexities are made even more difficult by the fact that different courts have interpreted "profits" quite differently. Barber [2] describes two prevailing generalities:

---

[2] Barber, William G. "Recovery of Profits Under the Lanham Act: Are the District Courts Doing Their Job?", *The Trademark Reporter*, Vol. 82 TMR, p. 141.

One view is that only those expenses which directly relate to the infringing product are deductible. Under this approach, only direct costs, such as cost of goods and direct labor, are typically deducted, and deduction of a proportional amount of overhead expenses will not be allowed unless defendant can show that such expenses increased due to production of the infringing product. This is the approach taken in the Third, Fifth, Seventh and Eleventh Circuits.[3]

The second view allows for a deduction of a portion of the defendant's general expenses, such as overhead, operating expenses, and federal income taxes. This more liberal approach is recognized in the Second, Fourth, and Ninth Circuits.[4]

---

[3] Century Distilling Co. v. Continental Distilling Co., 205 F2d 140, 98 USPQ 43 (CA 3 1953), cert denied 346 US 900, 99 USPQ 490 (1953) at 147, 98 USPQ 43 (court applied what it called the "differential cost or marginal profit theory"); Maltina Corp. v. Cawy Bottling Co. Inc. 613 F2d 582, 205 USPQ 489 (CA 5 1980) at 586-87, 205 USPQ 489 (only those costs which "actually relate" to the infringing product are deductible; Ruolo v. Russ Berrie & Co. 886 F2d 931, 12 USPQ2d 1423 (CA 7 1989), cert denied 110 S. Ct. 1124 (1990) ("variable costs" are deductible, "fixed costs" are not); Playboy Enterprises, Inc. v. P.K. Sorren Export Co. Inc. of Florida, 546 F Supp 987, 998, 218 USPQ 795 (SD Fla 1982) (following Maltina).

[4] W.E. Basset Co. v. Revlon, Inc., 435 F2d 656, 168 USPQ 1 (CA 2 1970), modf'g 305 F Supp 581, 163 USPQ 466 (SDNY 1969) at 665, 168 USPQ 1; Warner Bros., Inc. v. Gay Toys, Inc., 598 F Supp 424, 428-29, 223 USPQ 503 (SDNY 1984) (applying "full absorption approach" of accounting and rejecting "incremental approach"); Polo Fashions, Inc. v. Craftex, Inc., 816 F2d 145, 149, 2 USPQ2d 1444 (CA 4 1987) (court allowed deduction of total costs, but indicated that under different circumstances it might allow only marginal costs); O'Brien International, Inc. v. Mitch, 209 USPQ 212 (ND Calif 1980) (equating profits with "net taxable income"; court also held that a willful infringer may not deduct income taxes, citing L.P. Larson, Jr., Co. v. William Wrigley, Jr., Co., 277 US 97, 48 S. Ct. 449, 72 L Ed 800 (1928).

In an excellent article on the subject of monetary relief in trade-mark infringement cases, Koelemay[5] describes three profit calculation methodologies:

> Under the *differential cost* or *marginal cost* rule, deductions are allowed only for expenses that would not otherwise have been incurred "but for" the manufacture and sale of the infringing product. No deductions for fixed costs and overhead . . . would ordinarily be allowed . . . This rule results in the largest recovery for the trademark owners . . . Many recent trademark and patent decisions favor this approach. This approach has also been used for calculating the plaintiff's lost profits on lost sales.
>
> [This would appear to be equivalent to gross profit on an incremental accounting basis.]
>
> Under the *direct assistance* rule, all expenses which directly assisted in the manufacture and sale of the product can be deducted, including some items of overhead. This rule has also enjoyed wide support.
>
> [This might be equivalent to a net operating income measure with at least some element of full absorption accounting.]
>
> Under the *fully allocated cost* rule, all expenses properly allocable to the product under generally accepted accounting principles are allowed.
>
> [This appears equivalent to net income under fully absorbed accounting principles.]

---

[5]Koelemay, James M. Jr., "A Practical Guide to Monetary Relief in Trademark Infringement Cases," *The Trademark Reporter*, Vol. 85, May–June, 1995, No. 3, pp. 288–89.

We have not included the voluminous footnote references to this excerpt contained in Mr. Koelemay's article. Also, in a following section of his article, Mr. Koelemay lists specific expense items along with cases relating to their deductibility. The reader seeking additional guidance should refer to this source.

One could construct a chart that shows how various courts have applied the concept of awarding infringer's profits. A matrix of cases and courts would provide a hint of how to make the calculation based on past decisions. Such a matrix might not, however, be helpful in the long run. We tend to think of these situations in terms of an expert witness, called upon to opine, in an objective way, about the monetary effect of some action (i.e., trademark infringement). If the decision about what to deduct, or what accounting system to use is related to the degree of "willfulness or deception" exhibited by the infringer, or what different courts have decided in specific past cases, quantification becomes almost impossible. Whoever attempts this quantification is tempted to calculate a whole menu of possible profits measures so that the court can make its choice.

(b) Damages Sustained by the Plaintiff

Quantifying damages that may have been sustained by the plaintiff is a task that may include a calculation of sales (and profits) lost as a result of the infringement, royalties foregone because the infringer did not enter into a license, or the cost of "repairing" damage to the plaintiff's trademark.

(c) Plaintiff Lost Profits

If the defendant has launched a product or service that is directly competitive with the plaintiff's, the quantification of lost profits may be relatively clear. This situation ought to result in some deterioration of the plaintiff's sales (and profits). It may also be necessary to make an analysis of sales trends and market share in order to measure the effect of the infringing competition. Consideration may also have to be given to price cuts or other concessions that were given by the plaintiff in order to maintain sales levels in the face of this infringing competition. The objective is to measure the plaintiff's position before the infringement and compare it with the plaintiff's business after the infringement, eliminating the possible effects of unrelated exogenous influence.

In quantifying lost profits, many of the concepts discussed above come into play. The objective is to isolate the financial performance of the affected plaintiff product or service before and after the infringement, in order to measure the infringer's economic impact. The same tasks may have to be undertaken to make this isolation.

When the infringing product or service is unrelated in the marketplace to those of the plaintiff, evidence of lost sales is unlikely to be found, and the infringer's profits may be a more appropriate measure of monetary relief.

(d) Reasonable Royalty

The essence of this method of estimating plaintiff damages is the royalty that would have been received by the plaintiff, had the defendant negotiated a license agreement before the infringement began. We discuss trademark royalty rates elsewhere, as they would be on an arm's-length basis. There are those who might argue that the royalty rate used in damages awards should be higher than that evident in the market in arm's-length transactions, because the infringer should be penalized for not seeking a license in the first place. This is logical and has precedent, but we question whether it should be in the province of the expert to suggest to the court the magnitude of this punishment element. The expert should provide to the court an opinion of what is required in the marketplace.

This is not a trivial task, because true market transactions are few, the information about them is scarcer still, and knowledge about the degree of comparability is rarer yet. The biggest difficulty that we see is the difference between market royalty rates (which are payments for full use of property in some market segment) and a royalty rate that would be appropriate for whatever partial rights the infringer has usurped. In theory, market royalty rates would be most appropriate in a counterfeiting situation, where the infringer has taken all of the rights to a mark as an unauthorized licensee. In most infringements, only some elements of the mark have been usurped, and market royalty rates may not apply.

It may well be necessary, even desirable, to fashion a royalty using investment rate of return principles, which should yield a royalty rate that reflects the economics of the specific infringing transaction.

(e)   Repairing the Plaintiff's Damage

An alternative measure of plaintiff damages is what it would cost to repair whatever damage has been done to the plaintiff's trademark. This is basically an insurance concept to "make whole" the policy-holder. The most popular measure by this standard seems to be the cost of corrective advertising. It is assumed that the plaintiff, by employing advertising, can reverse whatever confusion exists in the mind of the buying public by advertising directed to that end. It is very difficult to estimate with any degree of precision the cost of such advertising. Pricing the necessary advertising is not so much a problem as estimating how much of what type of advertising is necessary to accomplish the objective. One rule of thumb (apparently from Federal Trade Commission litigation) is that 25 percent of the infringer's advertising expenditures will do the job. We are unaware of the theo-retical origins of this concept. Obviously, if there is confusion in the marketplace about the origin of goods or services because of infringe-ment, advertising is a tool that can be used to correct it. How much advertising, its type, and cost will vary widely, depending on the amount of confusion, the kind of confusion, and the economic impact of the confusion. It seems to us that it ought to be incumbent on the plaintiff to provide evidence that advertising is the most appropriate "repair" and, in addition, the type and cost of such advertising.

It may well be that the damage to the plaintiff is the loss of distributors, retail outlets, manufacturer's representatives, "shelf space," and the like. A plaintiff may have lost revenues related to ancillary services connected to the infringed product, or may be liable for future claims against infringing products out in the marketplace. Advertising is not a curative in this case. It may be necessary to add sales staff and incur other marketing costs in order to regain a former position.

11.4 SOME CASE EXAMPLES

We can observe how these concepts have surfaced in various instances of trademark infringement in the following discussion of specific cases.

(a) U-Haul International, Inc. v. Jartran, Inc.[6]

The issue was false comparative advertising. The U.S. District Court for the District of Arizona awarded plaintiff $40 million in damages plus a permanent injunction against future false advertising. On appeal to the U.S. Court of Appeals, Ninth Circuit, the decision was that the award, based on U-Haul's corrective advertising expenditures and revenue decline, was correct and that doubling these measures under the provisions of the Lanham Act was proper. This prevailed over the arguments by Jartran that the award was more than twice the amount of U-Haul's original advertising expenditures, and that Lanham Act provisions should not apply, since U-Haul's trademark was not registered with the patent and trademark office.

---

[6]U-Haul International, Inc. v. Jartran, Inc., 601 F Supp. 1140 (1984).

Jartran further argued that the District Court should not have included $6 million of its advertising campaign as "profits," because it did not make a profit during the relevant period. Jartran's profitability was considered by the Appeals Court to be irrelevant and found that the District Court's assumption that Jartran's financial benefit was at least equal to the advertising expenditures was not erroneous.

Measures of damages:

- U-Haul revenue decline due to Jartran ads = $20 million (taxes were not deducted).
- Jartran's ad campaign = $6 million plus U-Haul corrective advertising = $13.6 million. Total approximately $20 million.

Conclusion on damages:

- $20 million advertising expenditures doubled = $40 million.

(b) Big O Tire Dealers, Inc. v. Goodyear Tire & Rubber Company [7]

The issue was false designation of origin and common law trademark infringement relative to the BIGFOOT, trademark for automobile tires. The jury's decision in the United States District Court for the District of Colorado awarded the plaintiff general compensatory damages of $2.8 million and punitive damages of $16.8 million. The case was appealed and the United States Court of Appeals, Tenth Circuit, reduced general compensatory damages to $678,302 and punitive damages to $4,069,812. We found no specific claims of damages by the plaintiff, other than the assertion that advertising was the appropriate

[7] Big O Tire Dealers, Inc. v. Goodyear Tire & Rubber Co., 408 F Supp 1219, 1239, 189 USPQ 17 (D Colo 1976), modf'd and aff'd 561 F2d 1365, 1373, 195 USPQ 417 (CA 10 1977), cert dismissed 434 US 1052 (1978).

way to repair the damage to goodwill. The decision was by the jury, based on standards contained in the Court's instructions.

Measures of damages (District Court):

- The difference between the value of plaintiff's goodwill before and after the acts of the defendant.
- That the damages could be based on the plaintiff's contention that it would have to mount an advertising campaign to restore the BIGFOOT trademark to its condition before the defendant's actions.

Conclusion on damages (District Court): .

- Goodyear spent approximately $10 million on BIGFOOT advertising.
- Big O dealers were in 14 of 50 states.
- 14/50 = 28% × $10 million = $2.8 million.
- Punitive damages = 6 times compensatory damages
- $2.8 million × 6 = $16.8 million.

Conclusion on damages (Appeals Court):

- Goodyear's actual advertising expenditures were $9,690,029.
- 14/50, or 28% × $9,690,029 = $2,713,208.
- $2,713,208 times the Federal Trade Commission 25 Percent Rule for corrective advertising = $ 678,302.
- Punitive damages = 6 × $678,302 = $4,069,812.

(c) Zazu Designs v. L'Oreal S.A.[8]

This action, in the District Court for the Northern District of Illinois, was brought by the plaintiff in six counts, one of which was trademark infringement under Illinois statutory and common law. This is

---

[8]Zazu Designs v. L'Oreal S.A., 979 F2d 499, 24 USPQ2d 1828, 1835 (CA 7 1992).

an interesting case, in part because the court's annoyance with the actions of the defendant before and during the trial was clearly evident. The defendant claimed that it was the exclusive licensee (for use on hair cosmetics) of the ZAZU trademark which was federally registered as a mark for men's and boy's clothing. The plaintiff had minimal sales of the product prior to the infringing actions, as it was gearing up to introduce it to market.

Conclusion on damages (by the Court):

- $100,000 as "a measure of plaintiff's lost profits and defendant's infringing sales."
- Defendant's advertising and promotional expense was estimated at $5 million. $5 million times 20% = $1 million.
- Punitive damages equal to 5% of defendant's "economic strength" of $20 million = $1 million.

These damages were reversed on appeal by the Seventh Circuit.

(d)　West Des Moines State Bank v. Hawkeye Bancorporation[9]

The plaintiff brought this action for infringement of its WEST BANK service mark in the United States District Court for the Southern District of Iowa. It was appealed to the United States Court of Appeals, Eighth Circuit.

Conclusion on damages (District Court):

- Hawkeye advertising totaled $75,505.73.
- Using the FTC 25 Percent Rule, damages were calculated to be $18,876.43.
- No punitive damages.

Conclusion on damages (Appeals Court):

---

[9] West Des Moines State Bank v. Hawkeye Bancorporation, 722 F.2d 411 (1983).

- Of the $75,505.73 advertising expenditures of the defendant, $24,874.95 was spent for forms and supplies. Only the remainder, or $50,630.78 was expended on "products designed to reach out and affect the public mind. . . ."
- This smaller amount was the proper base for the 25 percent calculation and the district court was ordered to recalculate the award (presumably $50,630.78 × 25% = $12,657.70).

(e) Aetna Health Care Systems, Inc. v. Health Care Choice, Inc.

This was an action for trademark infringement in the District Court for the Northern District of Oklahoma related to the plaintiff's federally registered service mark CHOICE for its prepaid health care plan. Because of the nature of this mark, there is some interesting survey evidence relative to the likelihood of confusion. The damages issue is dealt with in a straightforward manner.

Conclusion on damages:

- Defendant spent "over $50,000" in advertising.
- Plaintiff will have to use corrective advertising to remedy the incorrect associations created by the defendant's use of the mark.
- Damages are calculated at 25 percent of advertising expenditures, or $12,500, using the FTC rule of thumb.
- Because it cannot quantify the plaintiff's lost profits, the court uses a 3× multiple to award total damages of $37,500.

(f) Bandag, Inc. v. Al Bolser's Tire Stores, Inc.[10]

The plaintiff's action alleged patent and trademark infringement and was brought in United States District Court for the Western District of

---

[10] Bandag, Inc. v. Al Bolser's Tire Stores, Inc., 750 F2d 903, 917, 223 USPQ 982, 991, 992 (CAFC 1984).

Washington. Appeal was taken to the United States Court of Appeals, Federal Circuit. The district court's decision that the mark was infringed and the issuance of an injunction was affirmed by the CAFC. The damages issue went differently.

Conclusion of damages (District Court):

- Damages in the amount of $36,212.38 were determined based on an estimate of the royalties that the defendant would have paid had it been a defendant franchisee.
- No award for lost profits was made.

Conclusion of damages (CAFC):

- Damages were $0, because the defendant usurped only a very small portion of the rights that would have been enjoyed by a franchisee. Injunctive relief is sufficient.
- The decision to award nothing for lost profits was affirmed.

(g) Boston Professional Hockey Association, Inc. v. Dallas Cap & Emblem Manufacturing, Inc.[11]

This action was brought by the hockey league and member teams to prevent an unauthorized emblem manufacturer from making and selling products with the league and team trademarks and service marks. The case was heard in the United States District Court for the Northern District of Texas, appealed to the United States Court of Appeals, Fifth Circuit, remanded to District Court, and again appealed.

Conclusion of damages (District Court):

- Grant of injunctive relief.
- No award of damages.

---

[11] Boston Professional Hockey Assn. Inc. v. Dallas Cap & Emblem Mfg., Inc., 597 F2d 71, 202 USPQ 536 (CA 5 1979).

Conclusion of damages (Court of Appeals):

- Found actions constituted infringement under Lanham Act and remanded case to district court for determination of damages.

Measures of damages (District Court):

- Defendant had offered plaintiff $25,000 for 3-year exclusive license to manufacture and distribute 3-inch emblems.
- Defendant had offered plaintiff $15,000 for a 3-year, non-exclusive license.
- Defendant's profits attributed to the infringement were $5,200.

Conclusion of damages (District Court):

- Defendant infringed for 4 years. 4/3 times the license offer × $25,000 = $33,000
- An additional $33,000 was added for damages due to the defendant's unauthorized manufacture of emblems larger than 3 inches.
- Total amount of damages ($66,000) was doubled (because of the "bad faith" of the defendant) to $132,000.
- Defendant's profits of $5,200 were added. Damages totaled $137,200.

Conclusion of damages (Appeals Court):

- Plaintiff already had an exclusive licensee, so these rights were unavailable to defendant. Therefore, damage calculation should have been 4/3 × $15,000 = $20,000.
- Doubling this amount to account for the larger emblems was proper, and so actual damages should be $40,000.
- Remanded again to District Court for reconsideration of the amount of additional damages to be awarded above the actual amount.

(h) Holiday Inns, Inc. v. Airport Holiday Corporation[12]

Motel corporation brought action against a former licensee who continued to use a trademark after the license was terminated. The United States District Court for the Northern District of Texas found for the plaintiff.

Measures of damages:

- Transient business at the motel was 30 percent of the total, the remainder being weekly business obtained by the management.
- Profits of the motel during the infringing period were $38,215.
- While the defendant was a licensee, the royalty fee was the larger of 15 cents per room night or 3 percent of room sales.
- Later, but during the period of infringement, the royalty fee was raised to 4 percent and an advertising fee of 1 percent was in effect.

Conclusion of damages:

- Damages were calculated on the basis of the 4 percent royalty and the 1 percent advertising fee applied to the room sales during the infringing period. The amount was $54,320 + $15,015 = $69,335.
- Only 30 percent of this amount is appropriate as damages because only the transient business was attributable to the use of the infringing identity. Therefore, actual damages were $69,335 × 30% = $20,800.50.
- Damages were trebled due to "flagrant and willful conduct" to $96,795.

---

[12] Holiday Inns, Inc. v. Airport Holiday Corporation, 493 F.Supp. 1025 (1980).

(i)   W.E. Bassett Company v. Revlon, Inc.[13]

W.E. Basset was a leading manufacturer of manicuring instruments under the TRIM trademark. Revlon's infringing product was a cuticle trimmer trademarked CUTI-TRIM. The Second Circuit court reversed the District Court's decision not to award a full accounting of Revlon's profits.

(j)   Maltina Corporation v. Cawy Bottling Co., Inc.[14]

In this infringement action, involving the CRISTAL beverage trademark, the United States District Court for the Southern District of Florida granted the plaintiff injunctive relief, awarded damages, and ordered the defendant to account for gross profit earned on infringing sales. On appeal, the United States Court of Appeals, Fifth Circuit ordered the defendant to account for its profits as a remedy for unjust enrichment, and reversed the decision to award actual damages.

Conclusion of damages (District Court):

- Actual damages were found to be $35,000.
- Gross profits of the defendant were calculated at $55,050. This represented total revenue less cost of goods sold.
- No deductions were made for overheads or other expenses (which would have resulted in a loss).

Conclusion of damages (Appeals Court):

- Actual damages found to be $0, due to lack of support for the $35,000 amount.

---

[13] W.E. Bassett Co. v. Revlon, Inc. 435 F2d 656, 662, 168 USPQ 1 (CA 2 1970), modf'g 305 F Supp 581, 163 USPQ 466 (SDNY 1969).

[14] Maltina Corp. v. Cawy Bottling Co. Inc., 613 F2d 582, 205 USPQ 489 (CA 5 1980).

- Gross profits of the defendant in the amount of $55,050 were affirmed.

(k)   Monsanto Chemical Co. v. Perfect Fit Products Mfg. Co., Inc.[15]

Perfect Fit marketed mattress pads filled with Monsanto's ACRILAN acrylic fiber together with inferior materials and identified them as ACRILAN filled pads. The District Court refused to award profits, but the decision was reversed by the Second Circuit, saying that Perfect Fit was "deliberately engaging in commercial piracy" and that a deterrent was needed.

(l)   Springs Mills, Inc. v. Ultracashmere House Ltd.[16]

Ultracashmere House's ULTRACASHMERE mark was judged to infringe Springs Mills' federally registered trademark ULTRASUEDE.

(m)   Century Distilling Co. v. Continental Distilling Co.[17]

In this case, only 25 percent of the defendant's profits were awarded because it successfully demonstrated that only that portion was attributable to the infringement.

---

[15] Monsanto Chemical Co. v. Perfect Fit Products Mfg. Co. Inc., 349 F2d 389, 146 USPQ 512 (CA 2 1965), rev'g 232 F Supp 493, 142 USPQ 259 (SDNY 1964), cert. denied 383 US 942, 148 USPQ 772 (1966).

[16] Springs Mills, Inc. v. Ultracashmere House, Ltd., 724 F2d 352, 221 USPQ 577 (CA2 1983), aff'g in part and rev'g and remd'g in part, 689 F2d 1127, 217 USPQ 298 (CA 2 1982).

[17] Century Distilling Co. v. Continental Distilling Co., 205 F2d 140, 95 USPQ 43 (CA3 1953), cert. denied 346 US 900, 99 USPQ 490 (1953).

(n) Wynn Oil Co. v. American Way Service Corp.[18]

The District Court did not award profits after finding that American Way's use of Wynn's X-TEND trademark was an infringement, based on its inability to ascertain profits on the infringing sales. The Sixth Circuit reversed that decision noting that the burden of apportioning profits is on the defendant.

(o) Roulo v. Russ Berrie & Co., Inc.[19]

After the expiration of a greeting card design license with Roulo, Russ Berrie brought out its own line of cards which was found to infringe. Profits in the amount of $4.3 million were awarded. The Seventh Circuit affirmed the award.

(p) Truck Equipment Service Co. v. Fruehauf Corp.[20]

Fruehauf was found by the District Court to have infringed TESCO's trade dress relating to the exterior design of a hopper truck trailer. The award of profits was twenty percent of the amount earned by Fruehauf in the states in which TESCO had rights on the basis that this was the amount attributable to the trailer's appearance. The Eighth Circuit judged that TESCO should receive all of Fruehauf's profits in the defining states.

---

[18] Wynn Oil Co. v. American Way Service Corp., 943 F2d 595, 19 USPQ2d 1815 (CA 6 1991) aff'g and rev'g and remd'g, 15 USPQ2d 1728 (ED Mich 1990).

[19] Ruolo v. Russ Berrie & Co. Inc., 886 F2d 931, 12 USPQ2d 1423 (CA 7 1989), cert. denied 110 S. Ct. 1124 (1990)

[20] Truck Equipment Service Co. v. Fruehauf Corp., 536 F2d 1210, 191 USPQ 79 (CA 8 1976), cert. denied 429 US 861, 191 USPQ 588 (1976).

11.5 COUNTERFEITING

Within the frame of reference noted above, counterfeiting, as a form of infringement, may offer the most similarity to the binary patent infringement situation. Various sections of the law define counterfeiting as using a "reproduction, counterfeit, copy or colorable imitation of a registered mark," or the use of a "spurious mark which is identical with, or substantially indistinguishable from, a registered mark." Counterfeiting is one form of obscenity that is easy to define and recognize.

Counterfeiting is a criminal offense in many of the developed nations of the world, even though, as we previously noted, the direct economic damage to the rightful trademark owner may be negligible (in terms of lost sales and profits). Certainly, however, the ill-gotten gains of the counterfeiter should be forfeit, with penalties.

> As Congress well knew in beefing up the legal sanctions for counterfeiting trademarks in 1984 . . . the sale of counterfeit merchandise has become endemic—perhaps pandemic . . . Treble damages are a particularly suitable remedy [when the violation is surreptitious] . . . confiscating . . . profits in cases in which he is caught will leave him with a net profit from infringement.[21]

Counterfeiting can be detrimental to the health and well-being of a trademark, since it is highly unlikely that a counterfeiter is going to produce and sell better-performing, higher quality goods than the originals. If the counterfeit goods are believed to be genuine by the buyer

---

[21]Louis Vuitton, S.A. v. K-Econo Merchandise, 692 F. Supp. 906, 8 USPQ2d 1609 (N.D. Ill. 1988), *rev'd sub nom.,* Louis Vuitton, S.A. v. Lee, 875 F.2d 584, 10 USPQ2d 1935 (7th Cir. 1989).

(because of appearance, price, or marketplace), then the ensuing "quality disappointment" will undoubtedly tarnish the mark in the mind of that buyer unless he or she realizes what has happened.

According to a recent news article,[22] the International Anticounterfeiting Coalition ("IAC") estimates that counterfeit products resulted in $200 billion in lost sales for U.S. companies in 1994. This is a 300-plus percent increase over their 1987 estimate of $60 billion. As reported by IAC, cut-rate prices go hand in hand with counterfeit goods:

ROLEX watch	$4,000 vs. $15–$35
CHANEL scarf	$300 vs. $10
GUESS jeans	$60 vs. $25
NIKE t-shirt	$17 vs. $16

Most legal action is directed at retailers who are served with injunctions or from whom counterfeit goods are seized. It would be more effective to put larger targets, such as wholesalers or manufacturers, out of action, but they are more difficult and more expensive to pursue.

Adelson's article relates the story of HUNTING WORLD, a luxury goods retailer, whose owner decided that "enough was enough" and now spends $6 million each year protecting its brands. This is a substantial amount, to be sure, but understandable when compared with the $100 million in lost sales suffered by the company in 1992, before its vigorous program was instituted. In a raid on two factories in Italy early in 1995, one-half million counterfeit articles were seized, bearing not only the HUNTING WORLD trademark, but those of GUCCI, CARTIER, and RALPH LAUREN as well.

---

[22] Adelson, Andrea, "Retail Fact, Retail Fiction," *New York Times*, September 16, 1995, p. 31.

On August 9, 1995, the Anticounterfeiting Consumer Protection Act of 1995 was made into law. Intended to strengthen the 1984 Anticounterfeiting Act, it extends the scope of federal authorities that can take part in law enforcement and seizure activities, and extends damages that can be claimed by the owner of a counterfeited brand. One wonders if this is enough, given the magnitude of worldwide manufacturing capabilities and the availability of advanced technology that can create a veritable flood of extremely difficult to detect counterfeit merchandise.

The Economic Impact Task Force of the International Trademark Association ("INTA") has reported that counterfeiting is especially severe among INTA members in the apparel, consumer products, food/restaurant products, personal care products, pharmaceutical, and sporting goods/toy industries.

Within our focus on the economic aspects of monetary relief, the counterfeiting situation carries with it the same requirements to quantify damages to the plaintiff and/or profits of the infringer. Whatever number flows from that analysis is subject to mandatory trebling.

11.6 SUMMARY

Considering the myriad issues connected with trademark infringement and the almost infinite number of types and degrees of infringement, we feel that it is very appropriate to bifurcate such proceedings. Without some guidance as to the character of the harm that has befallen the plaintiff, or the apparent economic benefit to the defendant, the quantification of monetary relief becomes a large menu of possibilities. The cost of preparing the menu can be large and its usefulness questionable.

12

Information Checklist

The following information should be collected for both the plaintiff and the defendant. The list is general and may require customization for specific cases. A brief reason for collecting each item is also presented.

1. Monthly sales information for the infringing and infringed product. Sales tax returns can be the source of this information. This information is used to identify the amount of infringed sales.

2. Sales journals or other records that are maintained to summarize annual sales for the infringing and infringed product. This information should be collected for periods before, during, and after the infringement period. Such information allows the identification of trends that can show the diminished sales from introduction of infringing sales.

3. Information showing the sales history by customer and/or distributors for the products in question. One use of this information is to identify customers and distributors that are common to both the plaintiff and the defendant.

4. Product pricing information including published list price documents and policies for allowing discounts to the list price. Comparison of this information for both the plaintiff and the defendant can show the effect of infringement on market prices. This information can be used to establish price erosion.

5. All analyses that show cost of goods sold and variances regarding the infringed and infringing products. This information is the first step in identifying lost profits.

6. All analyses that show a breakdown of fixed versus variable expenses for both cost of goods sold and operating expenses for

the subject products. This information is used for calculating lost profits.

7. Information showing product sales, in units and revenues, by product line for the years in question on a monthly basis, if available. This same information should be collected by customer account. The customer account information allows for an analysis that may show a relationship between sales of the patented product and other ancillary and complementary products (convoyed sales).

8. All of the information listed in numbers 1 through 7 should also be collected for products that are considered to be convoyed sales. This will allow for the calculation of lost profits on convoyed sales.

9. Identify the geographical area served by the infringer and all competitors in each area. This information is part of the effort to make a case for lost profits.

10. Develop a list of customers that the plaintiff would have expected to make sales to but for the infringer. This is part of the lost profits analysis.

11. All correspondence with major customers along with internal documents, (such as sales reports), that discusses contracts with major customers. Part of the benefit of having this information is to show sales that would have been made but for the infringement.

12. Income Statements showing gross profits and operating profits associated with the consolidated company and the division or business unit producing the products or services in question. Product line income statements should also be obtained if possible. Profit margins can be important for deriving a reasonable royalty rate and this information is useful for that purpose.

13. Balance sheets for the consolidated organizations and the divisions producing the products or services in question. Product line balance sheets should be obtained if possible. This information can be used if it is possible to conduct an investment rate of return analysis.

14. The 10K SEC filings for the year of infringement if either the plaintiff or the defendant are publicly traded. This information can be very helpful for understanding the companies involved in the lawsuit. Information in these filings sometimes discusses aspects of the industry, products, technology, competition, regulations, and the strengths and weaknesses of the companies involved in the lawsuit.

15. Business plans and forecasts for the business and the product line in question at the time of infringement. This should include capital expenditure plans that were approved at the time that infringing initiative was commissioned. Such documents help to establish the thinking of the parties at the time of infringement. This information is useful in deriving an appropriate royalty rate that reflects the hypothetical negotiation date previously discussed.

16. All documents that show or discuss an investment rate of return analyses that may have been conducted to justify the infringing business initiative. This also shows information that is pertinent to the hypothetical negotiation date and can also demonstrate the importance placed on the infringing product by the infringer.

17. Product brochures that describe the products in question. These brochures can show the importance of product features which can help determine the importance of the infringed invention to the overall product. Such information is useful to deriving a reasonable royalty rate.

18. License agreements for any technology of a similar nature, or the specific patent, including agreements between related parties unrelated parties and internal transactions. The information in these licenses can be important to supporting a reasonable royalty rate.

19. Identification of all other intellectual property and intangible assets associated with commercializing the product or service in question. When an investment rate of return analysis is conducted, this information is helpful to allocating the overall profits of the company among the assets used in the business.

20. Profit margin information about other product categories of the infringer and infringed. This information is important for comparison purposes and can sometimes show the extent of contribution derived from the infringed patent. Such information can help implement the Analytical Approach.

21. Information about royalties received by the patentee for the licensing of the patent in suit. This information can be useful for supporting a reasonable royalty rate.

22. Information about the plaintiff's established policy and marketing program to maintain its patent monopoly by not licensing others to use the invention or by gaining licenses under special conditions designed to preserve that monopoly. This information is used in assessing one of the Georgia-Pacific factors as used in deriving a reasonable royalty rate.

23. Establish the commercial relationship between the plaintiff and the defendant. Are they competitors? In what geographic areas? In what aspects of the industry? This information is useful in assessing lost profits and/or a reasonable royalty rate.

24. Information that shows any effect of selling the patented product in promoting sales of other products of the defendant; the existing value of the invention to the plaintiff as a generator of sales of its non-patented items; and the extent of such derivative or convoyed sales. This information can show that the infringement benefited the infringer by assisting in the sales of products beyond the infringing product. Such information can support a high royalty rate on the infringing product.

25. Copy of the infringed patent(s).

26. Information that establishes the profitability of the product made under the patent; its commercial success; and its current popularity for both the plaintiff and defendant. Besides the financial information already requested, copies of consumer surveys and technical reports can provide information for answering this question. Internal company documents are also useful for assessing

the commercial success of the subject product. All of this information is useful for supporting the royalty rate that is concluded.

27. Information about the utility and advantage of the patent property over the old modes or devices, if any, that had been used for working out similar results. Consumer surveys, product reviews and technical testing can also be helpful for answering this question. All of this information is useful for supporting the royalty rate that is concluded.

28. Information about the nature of the patented invention; the character of the commercial embodiment of it as owned and produced by the plaintiff; and the benefits to those who have used the invention. This information is also useful for supporting the royalty rate that is concluded.

29. Information about the extent to which the infringer has made use of the invention; any evidence probative of the value of that use.

30. Any information known by management or other sources about the portion of the profit or selling price that may be customary in the particular business or in comparable businesses to allow for the use of the invention or analogous inventions. While it has been previously acknowledged that such information is rarely available, the question is still worth asking.

31. Information regarding related products whose demand is in some form dependent upon or influenced by sales of the infringed product.

32. Information about related or unrelated products that are sold through the same marketing channel. Frequently, complimentary products round out a product line and thereby reduce transaction costs for a buyer.

33. Damages from price erosion resulting from lower market prices caused by the effect of the market entrance of the patent infringer. In a competitive market a new entrant who offers essentially the same product (in this case by virtue of infringement) as existing participants frequently gains market share by price competition.

By forcing market prices below pre-entrance levels, revenues for existing participants (i.e., patentee) are reduced, thereby resulting in lower revenues and lost profits. The extent to which this occurs represents damages from price erosion. As such, all information about product pricing and changes in pricing should be collected, especially internal memorandums that discuss price changes.

In making document requests, the following citations may prove helpful. *Remember that the author is not an attorney and makes no representation about having any expertise in the law.*

Sometimes discovery requests are responded to by criticism of the relevancy of the request. This happens when profit margin information is requested for un-patented products of the infringer. The information can be useful for implementing the Analytical Approach but a reluctant defendant might not wish to assist its opponent in such a manner. For discovery purposes, "any matter that bears on, or reasonably could . . . bear on, any issue that is or may be in [the] case" is relevant. *Oppenheimer Fund v. Sanders*, 437 US 340, 351 (1978).

Discovery about non-patented products such as sales and profits is clearly relevant. In *Paper Machine Converting Co. v. FMC Corp., 432 F. Supp. 907 (E.D. Wisc. 1977), aff'd, 588 F.2d 832 (7th Cir. 1978),* the court made it clear that a patentee's damages include the sales of products not covered by the patent when those sales are made possible by the sale of the infringing product. The U.S. Court of Appeals for the Federal Circuit has held that an award of damages based on such "convoyed sales" is "not barred" from inclusion in the calculation of lost profits. *See Beatrice Food Co. v. New England Printing & Lithographing Co. 899 F.2d 1171, 1175 (Fed. Cir. 1990).*

Many discovery requests focus on manufacturing and marketing capabilities. Others look for information about consumer research and demand for the product. All of these requests are valid for addressing the Panduit factors, previously discussed in Chapter 4. The Federal Circuit has adopted the Panduit criteria for establishing lost profits.

The criteria for lost-profits damages are (1) the demand for the patented product, (2) the plaintiff's ability to meet demand, (3) the absence of acceptable non-infringing substitutes, and (4) the amount of lost profits per unit. *Sensonics, Inc. v. Aeronic Corp.* 81 F.3d 1566, 1572 (Fed. Cir. 1996) (citing *Panduit Corp. v. Stahlin Bros. Fiber Works, Inc.* 575 F.2d 1152 (6th Cir. 1978).

Requests for product pricing information over the infringing period are relevant where price erosion is a possible source of damages. *Herbert,* 99 F.3d at 1119; *Minnesota Mining and Manufacturing Co. v. Johnson & Johnson Orthopaedics, Inc.* 976 F.2d 1559 (Fed. Cir. 1992) (District Court did not err by finding that the patentee could have raised prices but for infringer's sales); *Lam, Inc. v. Johns-Manville Corp.,* 718 F.2d 1056, 1983 (Fed. Cir. 1983). When the patentee has lowered its price for its product because of the pricing policy of the infringer, price erosion exists.

Of course, damages caused by infringement may also be measured by a reasonable royalty applied to sales of the infringing products. *See SmithKline Diagnostics, Inc. v. Helena Laboratories Corp.,* 926 F.2d 1161, 1163 (Fed. Cir. 1991); 7 Donald S. Chisum, Chisum on Patents Section 20.03 (1997); see also, *Georgia-Pacific Corp. v. United States Plywood Corp.,* 318 F. Supp. 1116 (SDNY 197), *modified,* 446 F.2d 295 (2nd Cir. 1970), *cert. denied,* 404 US 870 (1971).

13

Settlement

This chapter is written for plaintiffs and defendants and in many ways represents some of the best advice in this book. You should work hard at settlement, even when it looks fruitless. Leave the lawyers at home and meet with top executives and decision-makers of your adversary. Leave pride and egotism at home because the goal is to make a prudent business decision. The goal is to return the energies of top management to running the business. Infringement lawsuits are substantial distractions for key employees that could otherwise be spending their time helping your company compete in the marketplace.

Infringers should admit to themselves that they have committed a wrong and they should stand up and pay for making a mistake. Stop questioning the validity of the infringed patent. Stop degrading the value of the invention. Take responsibility for what happened and figure out a fair compensation for the mistake. When eight-year-olds are confronted with something they broke, their first reaction is to deny responsibility. In effect, they are saying, "I didn't infringe." After it is proven that they are responsible for the damaged item, they argue that the broken item was never important anyway. Their strategy is to deny and then degrade. Infringers must come to realize that this strategy does not work for eight-year-olds and it will not work for them.

Plaintiffs must also be realistic. The infringer caused lost sales, price erosion, lost royalties, and maybe even a lower stock price. Too often, however, plaintiffs start to believe that the infringement is the root of all evil. Every misfortune of any nature is attributed to the infringement. Realistically, maybe some of the lost sales were never going to the plaintiff, regardless of the defendant. Maybe the product price would have dropped without the defendant in the market. Maybe the plaintiff would have licensed the invention for a cross-license and not cash. Maybe the stock price dropped because of the sex scandal. Plaintiffs deserve to be compensated for their damage, but getting a competitors' head on a platter is not going to happen. Waiting for an unrealistic damage award is a waste of time that could be better spent building the business.

Litigation can costs more than the $1 million for your attorney. Experts must be hired, too. Most damaging though is the distraction of key management. Enormous amounts of time, energy, and emotional strain are the result of participation in infringement lawsuits. Every aspect of a product or service comes under scrutiny beginning with the research and development people and going through design, the patenting process, manufacturing, engineering, accounting, marketing, selling, distribution, strategic planning, and licensing policies. Both sides have the right to discovery. This requires the production of all requested documents and personnel. Millions of pages are involved and your key managers are the ones that must stop their regular business activities to respond to discovery requests. Later they will be asked to provide testimony about the documents that they supplied to the lawyers. Testimony requires travel, preparation with the attorneys, refocusing of energies, and emotional strain. Here is a very brief representation of the investigation of some key management functions.

Research	Questions will be asked to determine the actual source of inventorship and the amount of time and effort put into the invention. Lab books will be discovered and researchers will be questioned about every aspect of the invention. Alternatively, they could be spending their time inventing a new product.
Engineering and Design	This investigation might focus on the ability of an infringer to design around

the invention. Hypothetical alternatives will be discussed and substantial time may be needed to disprove designs that were dropped many years ago for good reasons that are hard to remember. Alternatively, these managers could be improving the manufacturing process to ameliorate material usage and augment profits.

Patent Attorneys

In this avenue of discovery efforts will be made to prove the patent is invalid. The word fraud may even come up in the deposition. Ancient history will need to be recalled and justification for past actions may be required. Alternatively, new patents could be filed for new inventions by the research department.

Manufacturing

This investigation looks to show that the claimed lost sales could have actually been manufactured by the plaintiff. This area of investigation also involves identifying costs on a fixed and variable basis. Production capacity is questioned. Alternatively, production utilization could be improved.

Accounting

All aspects of accounting for the sales, costs, and profits of the product involved in the lawsuit are explored. Old accounting reports must be studied so that questions can be answered. Draft reports must be reconciled with reports that were actually issued and used by management. Alternatively, accountants could be improving the flow of vital information for better management decisions and control.

Marketing

Customer accounts are identified, marketing decisions are questioned, pricing strategies are reviewed, and all aspects of marketing methods are put on the table. Alternatively, new marketing programs could be devised for capturing new market share.

Sales

Territories are discussed, commissions must be disclosed, and the methods used to sell the product are questioned. Alternatively, sales could be increased and customer loyalty could be reinforced.

Distribution

The nature of the distribution network is questioned and the access it gives to customers is investigated to show the accounts and sales that were lost. Alternatively, sales could be increased and customer loyalty could be reinforced.

Strategic Planning

Business plans and the people that prepare them are the focus of this investigation. The goal here is to show the importance of the infringing product to the future of the company that infringed. Old plans are dusted and draft plans must be reconciled with the final versions that management ultimately endorsed. Alternatively, new business strategies for meeting new opportunities could be devised.

Licensing   Licensing policies and the royalties paid by others and paid by you are investigated in order to indicate a royalty for use in damages calculations. Alternatively, new technology rights for implementing new products could be obtained.

Whether you are the plaintiff or the defendant, your key managers will be taken off-line to prepare for delivering documents and testimony. They will be questioned and stressed by attorneys and interviewed about the job they do. They will sometimes be forced to second-guess themselves. The process is especially difficult because the questions will likely center around events that occurred many years ago. The cost is more than the time that is lost. An emotional strain can tax the effectiveness of key management. Few managers want to be witnesses in court. This prospect hangs over them as the litigation proceeds. A solution to this substantial cost is to settle.

Remember, settlement is not supposed to make you happy and cure all of your business and personal problems. The goal is to put the lawsuit behind you and get back to competing in the marketplace. Plaintiffs want a fair price for the damage caused by the infringer and defendants want to pay only for the damage they caused. When plaintiffs realize that they realistically can prove only certain types and amounts of damages and defendants realize that they are going to have to pay something for their actions, the process is well on its way. Settlement is close at hand when both sides think the terms are despicable—when the plaintiff thinks the defendant is getting away with murder and the defendant simultaneously thinks the terms are highway robbery, then it is time to step-up the negotiation because a solution is near. Leave rivalries and personal prejudices out of the process. Settlement is an unemotional business calculation.

Another way to settle a patent lawsuit is to buy a majority interest in the opposing company. Recently Iomega Corp. purchased the French firm Nomai, S.A. The two were locked in a fight over Zip drive patents that Iomega was claiming as its sole intellectual property. Nomai said in a joint announcement with Iomega that it had begun to negotiate a settlement with Iomega and Nomai had agreed "Iomega patents, trademarks, copyrights, and trade secrets are valid and enforceable" and that the French firm "had reproduced certain Iomega protected software in reverse engineering work for use in the manufacture of its XHD and DUO cartridges without authorization from Iomega." Nomai had confirmed the back-engineering publicly to *Newsbytes* back in November during an interview (*Newsbytes*, November 24, 1997). Not surprisingly, Nomai eventually concluded "there was substantial evidence that a court may rule against it." In a recently announced deal, Iomega will pay Nomai shareholders 188 French francs per share, or approximately $21 million, for the majority interest. Then it will settle all outstanding litigation against Nomai. The purchase also includes a $3 million side arrangement for Iomega to purchase new technologies used by Nomai in making its XHD and DUO cartridges.

Sometimes an infringement lawsuit is predatory in nature. These suits go beyond using the United States legal system to protect intellectual property rights. Sometimes questionable patents are used to launch attacks on competitors with the goal of financial ruin for the competitor. Plaintiffs in such actions have run out of business strategies and have decided that they may get lucky in the courtroom and take out a competitor with a large damage award. Settlement can be difficult for a defendant in such cases. The plaintiff is not looking for an equitable solution to an infringer's mistake. They are looking to eliminate the defendant from the landscape. Settlement may still be possible, however, as weaknesses in the predatory lawsuit are revealed through discovery. As weaknesses become apparent, the defendant may want to take the predator to the mat as punishment for the predatory action. Make sure that such a decision serves long-term business interests. Settlement may be distasteful in these circumstances, but making a point may not be in the best interests of your business. Remember, eventually witless jackals die of their own actions.

14

Emerging Trends in Patent Infringement Damage Awards 1982–June 1997

by Julie L. Davis and Kathleen M. Kedrowski[1]

---

[1] © 1997 Arthur Andersen LLP. Ms. Davis is the Partner in Charge of Arthur Andersen's Intellectual Property Consulting Practice, headquartered in Chicago. Ms. Kedrowski is a Senior Manager in Arthur Andersen's Intellectual Property Consulting Practice in Chicago. This article is based upon a study initially performed by James J. Nawrocki, a Partner in Arthur Andersen's Intellectual Property Consulting Practice in Houston. The factual summaries provided herein have been included for illustrative purposes only. They do not reflect any opinions of the author or of Arthur Andersen LLP as to the proper measure of damages.

14.1 INTRODUCTION

It has been over fifteen years since the formation of the Court of Appeals for the Federal Circuit to hear all patent case appeals. In that time the attention given to patent lawsuits and their resulting awards has increased. It is not unusual to open a newspaper and read about a large judgment in favor of a patent owner or a settlement of a long-litigated case. There is also some debate over whether the recent Appellate Court decisions in Rite-Hite and other cases has impacted the awards.

Over the past several years, Arthur Andersen LLP has compiled a proprietary database of patent infringement damages decisions reported in The United States Patent Quarterly ("USPQ") or Lexis.[2] This proprietary database includes all decisions related to patent damages reported from 1982 through June 30, 1997.[3] The database is updated semiannually for all reported decisions involving monetary damage awards.

From 1982 to June 30, 1997, a total of 322 decisions involving monetary damage awards were reported. One hundred three of those decisions were later reversed (in full or in part) and, of the remaining decisions, only 198 reported the amount of the award. Even fewer cited the components of or the basis for the award. However, the information that is available does provide some guidance as to what factors the courts have relied upon in deciding damages issues.

---

[2] Those decisions reported in other publications or that came to our attention from correspondence from one or more of the litigating attorneys have been summarized in a chart presented later in this article. Their facts have not been included in the graphics presented elsewhere.

[3] Throughout this study, the 1980s time period runs from 1982 through 1989 and the 1990s time period runs from 1990 through June 1997.

14.2 GENERAL TRENDS

(a) Bench or Jury

Not surprisingly, the percentage of jury trials has increased in recent years as shown in Exhibit 14.1 (based upon court of original decision). In the 1980s, over 80 percent of all cases were bench trials. In the 1990s, bench trials accounted for less than 60 percent of the cases.

(b) Number of Patent Damage Cases by Year

While there is no clear trend in the frequency of cases awarding damages by year, the 1990s thus far shows a 15 percent increase in awards over the 1980s. Exhibit 14.2 shows the actual number of cases awarding patent damages in each of the years summarized. It also indicates the level of court awarding or affirming such amounts.

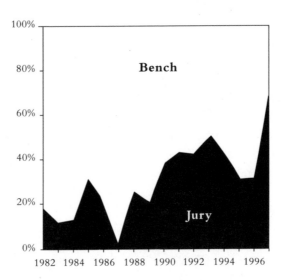

Exhibit 14.1   Breakdown of Cases
(© 1997 Arthur Andersen LLP)

Number of Cases

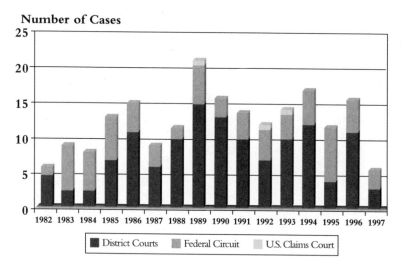

Exhibit 14.2   Patent Cases Awarding Damages per Final Jurisdiction (© 1997 Arthur Andersen LLP)

(c) District Court Awards (Excluding Polaroid)

When grouping the District Court awards by circuit, over 50 percent of the cases were tried in three circuits (Third, Seventh, and Ninth). The damage awards, however, appear to be disproportionate to the total number of cases tried, with the largest average award from the Sixth Circuit. (See Table 14.1.)

(d) Top Ten Awards

A look at the top ten damage awards in Table 14.2a shows that only three were awarded in the 1980s. If cases that have not yet been reported in the USPQ or Lexis are included (Table 14.2b), two interesting things occur: (a) only one award from the 1980s will remain, and (b) this elite club requires damages of $72 million, over 60 percent higher than the first graphic.

Table 14.1 District Court Decisions for the Period 1982–June 1997 (Excluding Polaroid)

Circuit Court	Number of Cases	Damages Awarded	% of Total		Average Award
			Cases	Damages	
First Circuit	4	$26,888,372	3%	2%	$6,722,093
Second Circuit	9	$122,320,797	8%	10%	$13,591,200
Third Circuit	22	$221,534,371	19%	18%	$10,069,744
Fourth Circuit	10	$33,792,561	8%	3%	$3,379,256
Fifth Circuit	11	$19,298,135	9%	2%	$1,754,376
Sixth Circuit	11	$242,361,581	9%	19%	$22,032,871
Seventh Circuit	15	$59,318,801	13%	5%	$3,954,587
Eighth Circuit	6	$48,824,662	5%	4%	$8,137,444
Ninth Circuit	22	$395,597,833	19%	32%	$17,981,720
Tenth Circuit	3	$1,714,771	3%	0%	$571,590
Eleventh Circuit	5	$77,969,463	4%	6%	$15,593,893

© 1997 Arthur Andersen LLP

Table 14.2a Top Ten Damage Awards

Case	Decision Year	Damages Awarded
Polaroid Corporation v. Eastman Kodak Company	1991	$873,158,971
Haworth Inc. v. Steelcase Inc.	1996	$211,499,731
Smith International, Inc. v. Hughes Tool Co.	1986	$204,809,349
3M v. Johnson & Johnson Orthopaedics	1992	$116,797,696
Fonar Corporation, et al. v. General Electric Co., et al.	1997	$103,421,726
Mobil Oil Corporation v. Amoco Chemicals Corporation	1994	$85,000,000
Stryker Corp., et al. v. Intermedics Orthopedics, Inc., et al.	1997	$72,750,704
Pfizer Inc. v. International Rectifier Corp.	1983	$55,805,855
Schneider AG v. SciMed Life Systems, Inc.	1994	$45,132,427
Shiley, Inc. v. Bentley Laboratories, Inc.	1985	$44,765,106

© 1997 Arthur Andersen LLP

Table 14.2b   Top Ten Reported Damage Awards*

Case	Decision Year	Damages Awarded
Polaroid Corporation v. Eastman Kodak Company	1991	$873,158,971
Haworth Inc. v. Steelcase Inc.	1996	$211,499,731
Smith International, Inc. v. Hughes Tool Co.	1986	$204,809,349
Stac v. Microsoft	*1994*	*$120,000,000*
3M v. Johnson & Johnson Orthopaedics	1992	$116,797,696
Celeritas v. Rockwell	*1997*	*$114,000,000*
Fonar Corporation, et al. v. General Electric Co., et al.	1997	$103,421,726
Mobil Oil Corporation v. Amoco Chemicals Corporation	1994	$85,000,000
Dow Chemical v. U.S.	*1996*	*$85,000,000*
Stryker Corp., et al. v. Intermedics Orthopedics, Inc., et al.	1997	$72,750,704

*Reported in USPQ and Lexis/*Reported elsewhere.*
© 1997 Arthur Andersen LLP

14.3 TOTAL AMOUNTS AWARDED

(a) Amount of Patent Damages Awarded by Year

It is no surprise that the awards have increased in recent years. The amount of that increase is startling, however. In the 1980s the total damages awarded/affirmed totaled approximately $600 million. In the 1990s, that total doubled to $1.2 billion. If the $873 million Polaroid v. Kodak case is included in the 1990 results, the total damages show a fourfold increase to over $2 billion. Exhibits 14.3 and 14.4 show the total damages awarded by year, with and without the Polaroid v. Kodak case (because the $873 million award tends to skew the results). Exhibit 14.5 shows the cumulative damages for the 1980s and 1990s.

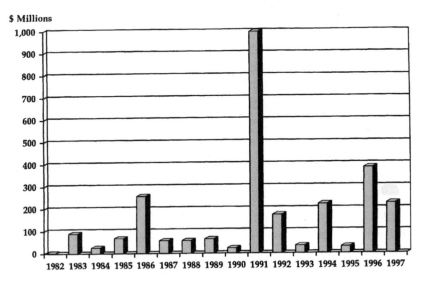

Exhibit 14.3   Total Patent Damages Awarded for the Period 1982–June 1997 (© 1997 Arthur Andersen LLP)

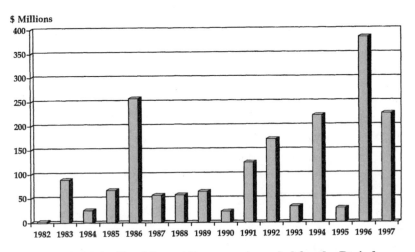

Exhibit 14.4   Total Patent Damages Awarded for the Period 1982–June 1997 (Excluding Polaroid) (© 1997 Arthur Andersen LLP)

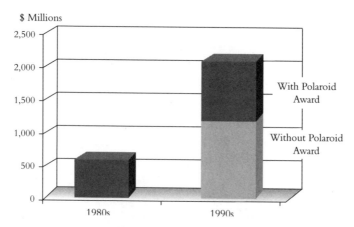

**Exhibit 14.5   Total Patent Damages Awarded for the Periods
1982–1989 and 1990–June 1997 (© 1997 Arthur Andersen LLP)**

(b)   Breaking the Awards Down into Bench v. Jury

You might expect to see a disproportionate share of the total dollars
awarded coming from jury trials. The facts do not clearly show this,
however. Exhibit 14.6 demonstrates that 30 percent of all the cases
studied were jury trials and of total dollars awarded, approximately
the same percentage (29 percent) were awarded by those juries. The
jury results are disproportionate (19 percent) when the totals are analyzed including the large Polaroid bench trial.

(c)   Maximum and Average Awards (Excluding Polaroid)

Over the past 15 years, bench trials have awarded the greatest amounts;
however, there has not been much increase in the bench's maximum
award between the 1980s and the 1990s ($205 v. $212 million). Juries
on the other hand, have more than doubled their greatest award from
the 1980s to the 1990s ($45 to $103 million). Additionally, the average

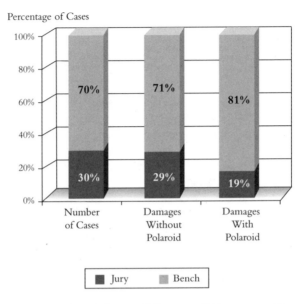

Percentage of Cases

**Exhibit 14.6   Breakdown of Cases and Damages—Bench
and Jury Decisions (© 1997 Arthur Andersen LLP)**

awards for both bench and jury have increased significantly from the
1980s to the 1990s. (See Exhibit 14.7.)

(d)   Range of Total Damages

Over the past 15 years, approximately 50 percent of the awards were
less than $1 million, with most of those decided by bench trials.
Exhibit 14.8 illustrates the ranges of the awards from 1982–June 1997.

A look at these ranges (see Exhibit 14.9) between the 1980s and
1990s, however, shows that more of the smaller awards (under $1 mil-
lion) occurred in the 1980s, whereas the majority of the larger amounts
(over $10 million) were awarded in the 1990s.

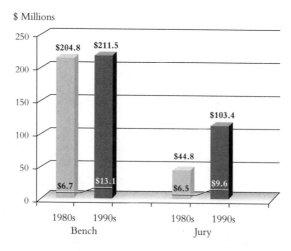

Exhibit 14.7   Maximum and Average Damage Awards (Excluding Polaroid) (© 1997 Arthur Andersen LLP)

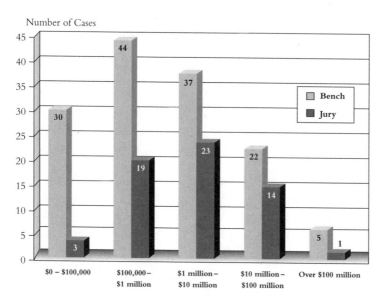

Exhibit 14.8   Range of Total Damages (© 1997 Arthur Andersen LLP)

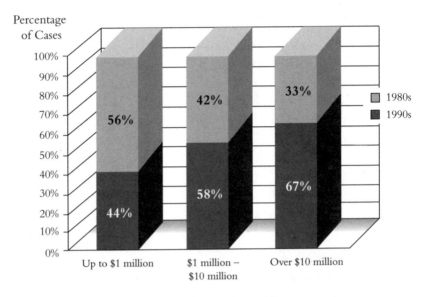

**Exhibit 14.9 Range of Total Damages
(1982–1989 and 1990–June 1997)
(© 1997 Arthur Andersen LLP)**

14.4 COMPONENTS OF DAMAGE AWARDS

(a) Breakdown of Patent Damages

Many of the damage decisions reported, particularly from jury trials, do not disclose the components that make up the total award. However, for those that do, reasonable royalty exceeds all other components as seen in Exhibit 14.10. Because the Polaroid decision includes $436 million of interest alone, it distorts this analysis. Excluding the Polaroid decision, as has been done in Exhibit 14.11, provides a better comparison of the true damage components and further highlights the prevalence of the reasonable royalty awards.

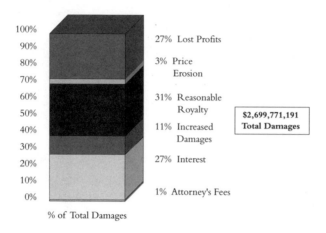

Exhibit 14.10 Breakdown of Patent Damages (All Cases Included) (© 1997 Arthur Andersen LLP)

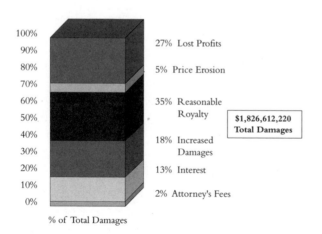

Exhibit 14.11 Breakdown of Patent Damages (Excluding Polaroid) (© 1997 Arthur Andersen LLP)

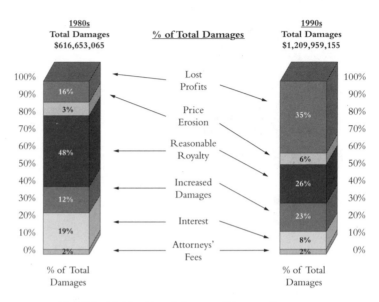

**Exhibit 14.12   Breakdown of Patent Damages
(Excluding Polaroid) (© 1997 Arthur Andersen LLP)**

(b)   Damage Award Components—1980s v. 1990s

Contrasting the components from the 1980s and the 1990s (see Exhibit
14.12) shows that reasonable royalty was the greatest component in
the 1980s, whereas lost profits was the greatest in 1990s.

(c)   Damage Award Components—Bench v. Jury

Studying the various damage award components separately for bench
v. jury decisions can be enlightening (see Exhibit 14.13). Before jump-
ing to conclusions though (e.g., juries are less likely to grant price erosion damages), keep in mind that the reporting mechanism, especially
as related to jury decisions, cannot capture all the factors that may
weigh into the ultimate award decision.

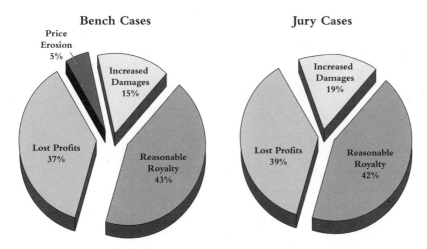

Exhibit 14.13   Components of Damage Awards—Bench and Jury Decisions (© 1997 Arthur Andersen LLP)

14.5   REASONABLE ROYALTY

(a)   Comparison of Reasonable Royalty and Lost Profit Cases

The previous exhibits have provided us with some understanding of how the amounts of damages awarded for royalties and lost profits compare. Now let's look at how prevalent reasonable royalty awards have been in terms of number of cases. (See Exhibit 14.14.)

Comparing the 1980s and 1990s (see Exhibit 14.15) shows a drop in reasonable royalty cases but an increase in combined reasonable royalty and lost profits cases.

(b)   Sources of Reasonable Royalty Rates

Within the court system, the appropriate royalty rate has been established in a variety of different ways. In the 67 cases where the basis of

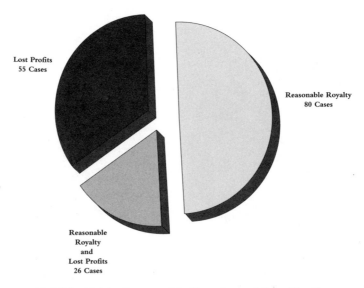

**Exhibit 14.14   Reasonable Royalty and Lost Profits
(© 1997 Arthur Andersen LLP)**

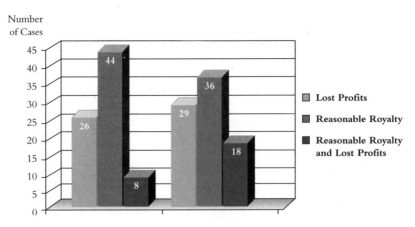

**Exhibit 14.15   Reasonable Royalty and Lost Profits
1982–1989 and 1990–June 1997 (© 1997 Arthur Andersen LLP)**

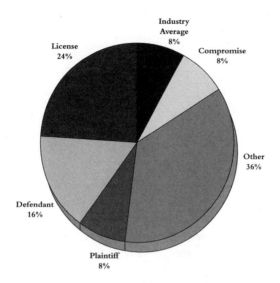

License
24%

Industry
Average
8%

Compromise
8%

Other
36%

Defendant
16%

Plaintiff
8%

**Exhibit 14.16   Sources of Reasonable Royalty Rates Breakdown
Per Number of Cases (© 1997 Arthur Andersen LLP)**

the royalty rate has been disclosed, about half of the decisions have relied upon an established royalty or the profit of one of the parties as shown in Exhibit 14.16. Juries established seven of the awards disclosing the source.

(c)   Reasonable Royalty Rates

The royalty rate percentages reported span a broad range as depicted in Exhibit 14.17. Clearly, though, the largest number of such cases have set a royalty rate in the five to twenty percent range.

(d)   Top Royalty Rates

The number of decisions involving royalty rates of 20 percent and over have grown over the past few years. The cases are listed in

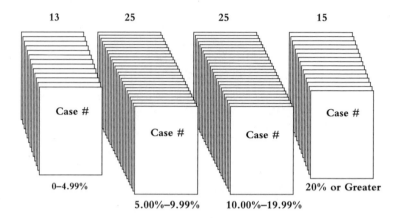

**Exhibit 14.17   Breakdown of Reasonable Royalty Rates
Per Number of Cases (© 1997 Arthur Andersen LLP)**

Case	Decision Year	Royalty Rate	Bench/ Jury
Hartness International v. Simplimatic Engineering	1987	70.00%	B
Williams v. Skid Recycling, Inc.	1994	35.00%	J
Trans-World Manufacturing Co., Inc. v. Dura Corp. and Kiddie	1986	30.00%	B
TP Orthodontics v. Professional Positioners	1992	30.00%	B
Additive Controls & Measurement Systems, Inc. v. Flowdata Inc.	1993	25.00%	B
Smithkline Diagnostics v. Helena Laboratories	1991	25.00%	B
Pentech International, Inc. v. Leon Hayduchok, et al.	1996	25.00%	B
Joy Technologies, Inc. v. Flakt Inc.	1996	25.00%	B
Bandag, Inc. v. Al Bolser Tire Stores, Inc.	1985	23.75%	B
DNIC Brokerage Co. v. Morrison & Dempsey Communications	1989	22.00%	B
Alm Surgical Equipment, Inc. v. Kirschner Medical Corp.	1990	20.30%	J
Water Technologies Corp. v. Calco Ltd.	1989	20.00%	B
CPG Products Corp. v. Pegasus Luggage, Inc.	1985	20.00%	Unknown
Minco, Inc. v. Combustion Engineering, Inc.	1996	20.00%	B
Gasser Chair Co. v. Infanti Chair Manufacturing Co.	1996	20.00%	B

**Exhibit 14.18   Royalty Rates Over 20 Percent for the
Period 1982–June 1997 (© 1997 Arthur Andersen LLP)**

Exhibit 14.18. In most, the royalty base is the defendant's net sales. You may note that four of these cases were decided in 1996, more than in any one year previously.

14.6   INTEREST RATES

(a)   Range of Interest Rates

The reported decisions also provide a basis to compare interest rates used in calculating prejudgment interest awards. In terms of magnitude, the largest number of cases involved rates in the ten to eleven percent range as shown in Exhibit 14.19.

(b)   Source of Interest Rates

Given the range of interest rates prevailing during the 1980s, the previous analysis by itself is not particularly revealing. A more useful analysis is to understand the source of these rates. As Exhibit 14.20 shows, the U.S. prime rate has most often been selected as the basis for prejudgment interest.

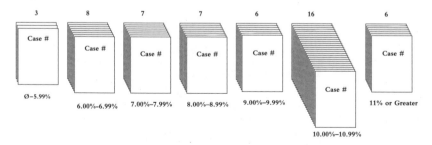

Exhibit 14.19   Interest Rate Breakdown Per Number of Cases (© 1997 Arthur Andersen LLP)

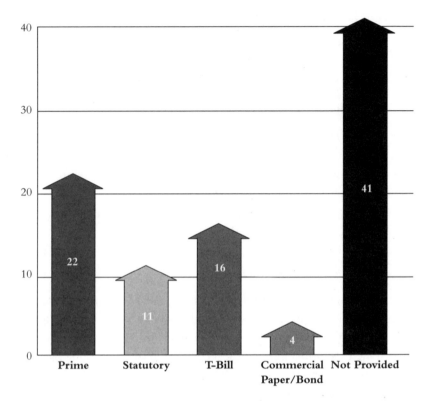

**Exhibit 14.20   Source of Interest Rate
Breakdown Per Number of Cases
(© 1997 Arthur Andersen LLP)**

(c)   Trends in Interest Rate Sources

A closer look at the information available to us on the interest rate
sources is even more intriguing. We learn, for instance, that the commercial paper rate has only been selected by the trier of fact in the
1980s. Also, as Exhibit 14.21 shows, the reliance on U.S. prime and
T-bill rates has been growing in the 1990s.

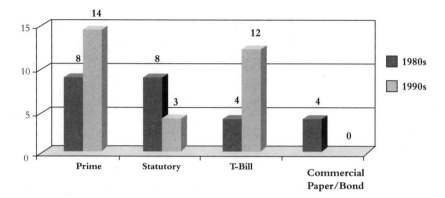

**Exhibit 14.21   Sources of Interest Rates Breakdown
Per Number of Cases (1982–1989 and 1990–June 1997)
(© 1997 Arthur Andersen LLP)**

14.7   INCREASED DAMAGES

(a)   Breakdown of Increased Damages

Nearly one third of all decisions since 1982 have included an award of increased damages. Of those cases involving increased damages (see Exhibit 14.22), potential infringers should note the large number resulting in trebled awards.

(b)   Multiple of Increased Damages

Of all the cases awarding increased damages, 66 percent of them followed bench trials. Interestingly, as Exhibit 14.23 illustrates, bench trials were more likely to end with trebled awards than another smaller multiple. Jury trials, on the other hand, more often resulted in a doubling of the damages awarded.

Exhibit 14.22   Cases of Increased Damages Per Type of Increase
(© 1997 Arthur Andersen LLP)

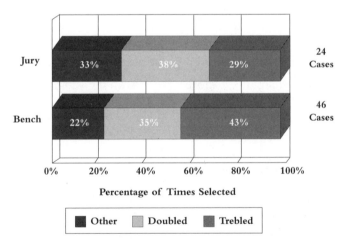

Exhibit 14.23   Increased Damages—Bench and Jury Decisions
(© 1997 Arthur Andersen LLP)

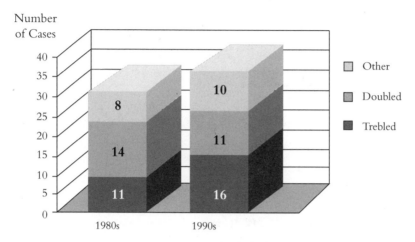

Number
of Cases

Exhibit 14.24 **Cases of Increased Damages Per Type of Increase**
1982–1989 and 1990–June 1997
(© 1997 Arthur Andersen LLP)

(c) Trends in Increased Damages

As Exhibit 14.24 shows, the occurrence of trebled awards has
increased in the 1990s while doubled awards have decreased. A further
look at the enhanced awards over time (Exhibit 14.25) shows a shift in
the selection of the multiple. It appears the jury's guidance on willfulness issues in the 1990s has impacted the ultimate selection of the multiple towards trebled sums. Without the jury's guidance, judges appear
to have elected to double sums in recent years.

14.8 APPELLATE DECISIONS

You may wonder how patent damage awards have fared on appeal. As
discussed previously, all those decisions involving awards that were
reversed, vacated, or remanded have been excluded from the analyses

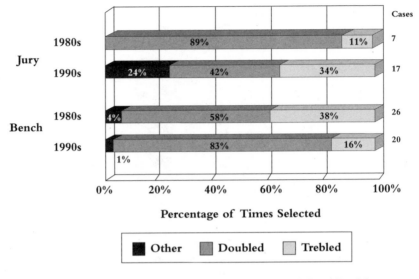

performed in the preceding exhibits. Looking back, though, at the total number of patent damages ever awarded can be disappointing to some patentees because many of the decisions have not stood up on appeal (as Exhibit 14.26 illustrates).

In the 1980s, over 60 percent of the components stood on appeal. In the 1990s, slightly over 50 percent were affirmed.

14.9   SUMMARY

The analyses described in this article shed some light on the decisions courts have made on patent damage awards as well as how these awards

Number of Cases

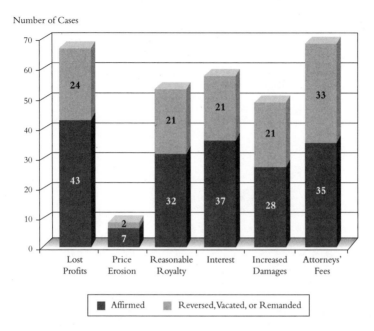

**Exhibit 14.26 Appellate Decisions by Damage
Type Per Number of Cases (© 1997 Arthur Andersen LLP)**

have changed over time. At the same time, though, these analyses elicit additional questions. How do settlement amounts compare? What is the difference between amounts awarded and those sought? How often are injunctions granted? The list of questions goes on and on. Unfortunately, due to confidentiality concerns and the lack of publicly available information, we may never know the answers to these questions and others.[4]

---

[4]If you would like to report other patent damage awards, components, settlement amounts, and settlement agreements, please send this information to Kathleen M. Kedrowski, Arthur Andersen LLP, 33 W. Monroe Street, Chicago, Illinois 60603.

APPENDIX A

Theory of Investment Rate of Return

Economic returns must be determined with consideration for the:

- amount of the returns
- form in which they will be provided
- timing of the returns
- trend expected in the amount of returns
- duration of the economic returns
- risk of receiving the returns

A comprehensive discussion of modern investment theory goes beyond the scope of this book. Complete books and careers are dedicated to the study of the relationship between risk and return. This appendix has been included to acquaint the reader with the basic concepts of risk and return and the vital role that these concepts play in determining the value of intellectual property and proper royalty rates. A bibliography provides books and articles that should be studied to further appreciate the relationship between risk and return.

A.1 INVESTMENT RISK

Investment risk, whether that of a stock portfolio or an investment in intellectual property, is comprised of four broad components:

- Purchasing Power Risk
- Interest Rate Risk
- Business Risk
- Market Risk

Investors expect a return on all investments and require compensation for the various components of risk.

(a) Purchasing Power Risk

Even if the expected stream of economic benefits from an investment could be determined with absolute certainty, risk still exists with regard to the purchasing power of the future dollars that are received. There always exists the risk that inflation will intensify and consume any gains that may be realized from investment performance.

During the past few years inflation has run at only 2 percent. If a steady and level inflation rate could be expected to continue in the future, then investment planning could include an element in the rate of return requirements to assure that this amount of inflation were incorporated into the contemplated investment returns. In a sense, the purchasing power risk would be eliminated. Unfortunately there were periods within the fifty-year span with unanticipated swings of inflation. It is the unanticipated changes that introduce investment risk.

(b) Interest Rate Risk

This risk element presents uncertainty similar to purchasing power risk. Alternate forms of investment such as corporate bonds, treasury securities, and municipal debt provide another investment opportunity with which an intellectual property investment must compete. If the future brings with it higher returns than are available from investments of lesser risk, then the value of the intellectual property investment may be diminished.

(c) Business Risk

This element of risk is very specific to the company or intellectual property that is being studied. It involves the ability of a company to maintain customer loyalty, to achieve enough earnings to meet operating and debt expenses, to meet competitor challenges, and ultimately, to bear the risk associated with achieving a return for the equity and debt investors. Incorporated into this element of risk are business-cycle risks associated with specific industries, product liability obligations, and workforce harmony.

A very significant business risk pertaining to technological intellectual property involves the existence of competitive technology that may soon emerge. Remaining economic benefits that can be derived from the existing technology may be cut short by superior technology. This risk could limit the time frame over which initial investments are recovered.

(d)   Market Risk

A unique and often unkind element of risk is, in large part, associated with "market psychology." Irrespective of any fundamental changes in the expected performance of an investment, market risk reflects the fluctuation in the demand for a specific type of investment. On October 19, 1987, the stock market plunged in value by over 500 points as measured by the Dow Jones Industrial Average. The plunge was predicated by neither a fundamental change in economic outlooks nor the declaration of a world war. Yet the value of all investments dropped. This is indeed an example of market risk.

A.2   REQUIRED RATE OF RETURN COMPONENTS

There are three primary components integrated within the required rate of return:

- Risk-Free Rate
- Expected Rate of Inflation
- Risk Premium

The risk-free rate is the basic value of money, assuming there is no risk of default on the principal and the expected earnings stream is guaranteed. Under this scenario the investor has only sacrificed the use of the money for a period of time. Typically, the rate on long-term U.S. treasury securities serves as a benchmark for the risk-free rate. Because investors are interested in a real rate of return, a portion of the required rate of return must include an amount that is sufficient to off-set the effects of inflation. Therefore, the rate of return at which long-term treasury securities have been traded to yield represents two components of the required rate of return: the real risk-free rate and the expected inflation rate. On July 10, 1998, the Federal Reserve Bank of St. Louis reported that the average rate provided by long-term U.S. treasuries was 5.6 percent. Assuming that the long-term outlook for inflation is expected to be 3 percent then the real, risk-free rate of return that is demanded by investors is presently about 2.6 percent. Unfortunately, most investments are not risk free and must provide additional return to compensate for the risks that are associated with business risk. This is typically referred to as the risk premium. It represents compensation for the possibility that actual returns will deviate from those that are expected. Evidence easily can be found that higher rates of return are required where higher levels of risk are present. By focusing on the yield that is provided by different fixed-income securities, this principle can be demonstrated. The table below compares the yield on selected investments as reported by the Federal Reserve Bank of St. Louis on July 10, 1998.

Comparative Investment Returns	
Investment	**Yield %**
U.S. Treasury Bill (3 month)	4.95%
U.S. Treasury Bill (1 year)	5.07%
U.S. Long-term Treasury Securities	5.60%
U.S. Corporate Bonds, rated Aaa	6.48%
U.S. Corporate Bonds, rated Baa	7.08%

The yield differential between the 3-month and 1-year treasury bills represents the risk associated with purchasing power losses because the U.S. Government guarantees the safety of principal and interest in both cases. Treasury securities and two corporate bond issues with different ratings represent the long-term fixed-income securities. While they are all subject, for the most part, to the same purchasing power risks, the safety of principal and interest is different. The higher the risk, the higher the rate of return that investors expect. The corporate bonds rated Baa are the riskiest investment vehicles included in the table and they also provide the highest amount of investment return as compensation for the additional risk.

A.3   RATE OF RETURN MODELS

Having discussed the factors that affect rates of return and the components of investment returns, a review is provided of a variety of methods used to determine appropriate rates of return for use in evaluating intellectual property and royalty rates.

Briefly described are four different approaches that are used as a means to develop a required rate of return. They are:

- Dividend Growth Model
- Built-up method
- Capital Asset Pricing Model
- Venture Capital

(a)   Dividend Growth Model

The formula for determining the value of a share of preferred stock presents a simple version of the dividend growth model:

$$\text{Value} = \frac{\text{Dividend}}{\text{Required Rate of Return}} \qquad \text{(Eq. A.1)}$$

The dividend stream is known with certainty, having been contractually set. It is promised to continue into perpetuity at the established level. This eliminates the complex assignment of trying to determine the rate at which the dividend will grow. The growth rate is zero. If the value of the preferred share of stock is known and the dividend is known, then the equation is easily solved for the unknown value and provides an indication of the required rate of return.

$$\text{Required Rate of Return} = \frac{\text{Dividend}}{\text{Value}} \qquad \text{(Eq. A.2)}$$

The resulting rate of return is that which investors are seeking for investments that provide a fixed dividend into perpetuity, possessing characteristics of risk similar to the specific issue being valued.

Preferred stock is not without risk. The dividends are paid only after debt obligations are satisfied. The indicated rate could be used as a benchmark for any investment that promises a fixed cash flow stream into perpetuity, possessing the same characteristics of risk and to the same degree (this model also assumes the risk that the preferred shares will be called by the issuing corporation does not exist).

Application of the dividend growth model to common stock is more complex but, if properly applied, can provide a meaningful indication of the required rate of return for equity investments with certain characteristics of risk. In the case of common stock, the future level of the cash streams and the rate at which they might grow is not known with certainty. Expansion of the model used to evaluate preferred stock is presented below:

$$V = \frac{D1}{(1 + i)} + \frac{D2}{(1 + i)^2} + \frac{D3}{(1 + i)^3} \qquad \text{(Eq. A.3)}$$

where:

    V = the value of the common stock

    D = the amount of dividend during each successive time period

    I = the required rate of return on the stock

The value of the stock is presented as the discounting of all future dividends. Rather than attempt to determine the amount of dividends that will be paid in each future year, an assumption is generally made regarding the rate at which the current dividend will grow. Introduction of this factor into the model along with algebraic wizardry provides a useful form for the dividend growth model:

$$V = \frac{Do(1 + g)}{i - g} \qquad \text{(Eq. A.4)}$$

The value of the stock is related to the growth of the current dividend, Do, at the growth rate, g, capitalized at the required rate of return, i. If the value of V, Do, and g can be determined then the required rate of return, for an equity investment possessing comparable characteristics of risk, can be derived.

An important assumption is that the growth rate selected will be constant into the future. Also, the growth rate must be a value that is less than the required rate of return. This last requirement may seem to be too restrictive. What about a company that is growing at a fantastic pace? If the growth rate is indeed going to continue at the fantastic rate indefinitely, then the dividend growth model is not useful. It is important, however, to be realistic. The likelihood of being able to sustain abnormally high growth rates forever is small.

In many cases where reasonable estimates can be made for the value of the investment and the growth rate of the cash flow, an indication of the required rate of return can be calculated. The dividend growth model is most useful for defining appropriate rates of return for intellectual property that is close to the mature portion of its economic life and has already been proven commercially viable. At this point of the life cycle, future growth rates are more predictable and the overall market for the product or service with which the property is associated is well defined. One of the other rate of return models may turn out to be more appropriate for fast-emerging intellectual property.

(b) Built-Up Method

This method is very subjective but can be used to directly reflect the amount of risk inherent in the major risk factors discussed. The method lists each of the components of risk and assigns an amount of return to compensate for each risk component. An example is presented below.

The built-up method is quite attractive because it addresses each of the risk components individually and can reflect an individual investor's own perceptions of the relative degree of risk presented by each of the components. Unfortunately, quantification of the exact amount of return that is necessary to compensate for each risk component is not possible. Too much conservatism in setting the rates can make an otherwise viable investment appear too risky. A rosy outlook

Built-up Rate of Return	
Risk Component	**Required Return**
Risk-free Rate of Return	3.0%
Purchasing Power	1.5%
Market Risk	2.0%
Interest Rate Risk	1.0%
Business Risk	6.0%
Total Required Rate of Return	13.5%

can encourage investment in a project that will yield a return that is too low in relation to the accepted risk.

The built-up method is rarely used because of the unreliability associated with the setting of specific rates. However, it is useful in demonstrating the basic concept behind investment rate of return requirements. It lists the broad categories of investment risk and shows the amount of investment return that is needed to compensate for accepting each type of investment risk.

(c)   Capital Asset Pricing Model

The capital asset pricing model (CAPM) is one of several factor models. These models associate the proper rate of return to various investment factors. In the case of CAPM, the appropriate rate of return is determined by one factor—the volatility of investment returns relative to the investment returns that can be achieved by a broad market portfolio. The equation that describes the model is as follows:

$$Re = Rf + B(Rm - Rf) \qquad\qquad \text{(Eq. A.5)}$$

where:

Re = The equity rate of return

Rf = The risk-free rate of return

Rm = The rate of return provided by the overall market portfolio of investments

B = Beta, a measure of the volatility for a specific investment relative to the market portfolio

Application of CAPM is traditionally associated with assessing the risk and return for specific stock positions taken by investors. The risks and return of a particular stock are related to its asset base, industry position, and competitor attacks, as well as changes in inflation and other economic forces. The Capital Asset Pricing Model can be used to estimate the required rate of return for specific intellectual property by analyzing the required rates demanded by investors on specific stocks that operate in the same industry as that of the intellectual property. Analysis of a company's stocks that are dominated by the type of intellectual property being studied will more directly reflect required rates of return for intellectual property in specific industries.

CAPM and Beta.   Beta is a measure that indicates a company's susceptibility to changing conditions. These changes include inflation rate trends, monetary policy, world oil prices, and other factors that affect the rates of return on the entire market. Beta is a broad measure of the amount of risk inherent in a specific investment when compared to the diversified risk of a broad market portfolio.

If the stock of a company fluctuates more than the price of the broad market portfolio then the stock, and the underlying business assets, are more susceptible to macroeconomic shifts than a broad market portfolio. If the stock's price over the past is more stable than the broad market then the stock is considered less risky. A common stock that has a beta of 1.0 moves in perfect unison with the overall broad market. If the market rises by 10 percent then the specific stock with beta equal to 1.0 will also rise 10 percent. This stock is no more or less volatile than the broad market. Where beta is less than 1.0, the underlying stock moves in the same direction as the market but to a smaller degree and is less volatile than the overall market and less risky. Where beta is greater than 1.0, the underlying stock moves in the same direction as the market but to a larger degree and is more volatile than the overall market and is riskier.

Beta values are calculated for specific stocks by many investment advisory services and brokerage houses such as Merrill Lynch, Value Line, Standard and Poors, and *The Media General Financial Weekly*. A risk measure for valuing intellectual property can be determined by studying the betas of publicly traded companies that are highly dependent upon the same type of intellectual property for which a value is desired. If the risk of comparable and public companies in the same industry is the same as those affecting the subject intellectual property, then a study of their betas can serve as a risk benchmark.

CAPM and Ibbotson Associates, Inc. The studies conducted annually by Ibbotson Associates, Inc. have examined total long-term returns as comprised of dividends, interest payments, and capital appreciation. The investments studied include all New York Stock Exchange stocks, corporate bonds, and U.S. Treasury securities; bonds, bills, and notes. Using these studies, the return from investment in a broad market portfolio, Rm, can be determined for insertion into the CAPM model.

(d) Venture Capital

So far this appendix has discussed how to determine appropriate rates of return for an equity investment where risk quantification is possible by comparative analysis. CAPM is typically used where commercial viability of the investment is either already proven or highly likely. Rates of return for investments possessing similar risk characteristics serve as the basis for development of an appropriate rate. Investments in emerging technology carry much higher risks with considerable potential for complete loss of the initial investment. In addition to the risks previously discussed such as inflation, competition, changing economic climates, and the like, emerging technology carries additional risks. Additional risks include the possibility that laboratory-scale success may not survive the transition to pilot plant production, or that pilot plant scale successes may not be economically successful at full-scale levels of commercial production. Embryonic technology investments may not even be defined past the pencil and paper stage of development where laboratory experimental success isn't even assured.

These types of intellectual property investments involve substantial risks and investors expect substantial "pay days" if the commercial viability ever materializes. The seed money for such risky investments are provided more and more by venture capitalists. Sometimes the word "venture" is replaced with "vulture" because of the seemingly extraordinary rate of returns that these investors require. But, considering the high potential in these cases for the total loss of millions of dollars of seed money, the required investment returns aren't really out of line.

At various stages of development, the venture capital required rate of return changes with the amount of risk that is perceived at each stage. Presented below is an estimate of the amount of return required at different development stages:

Venture Capital Rates of Return	
Stage of Development	Required Rate of Return
Start-up	50%
First Stage	40%
Second Stage	30%
Third Stage	25%

The various levels of venture financing can be expressed as follows:

Start-up. Start-up is a company with an idea and not much else. This is the riskiest level of embryonic intellectual property investment and requires the largest amount of return. The funds are used for basic research and possibly development of a prototype. At this stage, revenues are not even part of management goals.

First Stage. First Stage companies may have a prototype that has proven its capabilities but further development is required before commercial scales of production can be achieved. Positive net cash flows may still be several years away.

Second Stage. Second Stage companies may have experienced success in the commercial production of the product or service but expansion of market penetration requires substantial amounts that a bank may be unwilling to provide. At this point, the ability to make a profit may be already proven but rapid expansion requires more than present operations can provide.

Third Stage. Third Stage financings begin to blur with fast growth companies that can get limited bank loans or additional funds from a public offering. Strong profit levels may be consistently achieved but more funds are needed for national or global expansion.

A specific industry example considered here is the drug industry. Hambrecht and Quist, a venture capital investor, uses the following investment rate of return requirements for discounting cash flows derived from commercialization of biotechnology and pharmaceutical technology. Ashley Stevens of Boston University Community Technology Fund discussed these rates at a Licensing Executives Society conference in Orlando, Florida. The table below shows how the rates are related to the risk of different biotechnology and pharmaceutical projects.

Hambrecht & Quist	
Development Stage	Rate of Return Requirements
Discovery	80.0%
Preclinical	60.0%
Phase I Clinical Trials	50.0%
Phase II Clinical Trials	40.0%
Phase III Clinical Trials	25.0%
New Drug Application	22.5%
Product Launch	15–17.5%

After product launch the remaining categories of business risk begin to fall into categories that are typical of ordinary businesses. Rapid growth products and mature products carry investment risk that can be quantified by performing a weighted average cost of capital analysis as previously discussed.

Venture capital companies are not long-term investors. They typically try to get out of the investment in five to seven years with a three- to ten-fold increase in the original investment. This is usually accomplished by selling the interest in the developed company to a larger corporation or taking the developed company public.

A.4   WEIGHTED AVERAGE COST OF CAPITAL

The discussion thus far has presented various concepts and methods that help define the rate of return on equity investments. However, investments are usually financed by a combination of equity and borrowed funds. Corporate investments typically must pass hurdle rates in order to be considered as viable opportunities. Because debt and equity funds are used to finance these investments, the return provided must be sufficient to satisfy the interest due on the debt and also provide a fair rate of return on the equity funds. The hurdle rate must be this weighted average cost of capital, at a minimum.

A corporation that is financed with both debt and equity might have a capitalization structure that is comprised of 25 percent debt and 75 percent equity. A good bond rating might allow the corporation to finance debt at 6.5 percent. An appropriate equity rate, as determined from one of the models above, might be 13 percent. Shown below is the weighted average cost of capital. The tax deductibility of interest expense makes the after-tax cost of debt only 60 percent of the stated interest rate for corporations that pay a combined state and federal income tax of 40 percent. Equity returns are in no way tax deductible. When the cost of these capital components are weighted by their percentage of the total capital structure, a weighted average cost of capital of 9.98 percent is the result. This is the amount of return that the company must earn on its investments.

A multinational corporation, for which a 9.98 percent weighted average cost of capital is appropriate, may be a well-diversified "basket" of investments. Some of the investments may be more risky than others. Overall, the rate of return that these investments must earn is 9.98 percent.

If we apply this concept to a small company, or an isolated subsidiary of a multinational company, the weighted average rate of return requirement can also be allocated among the assets that are employed within the defined business enterprise. The allocation is conducted with respect to the amount of investment risk that each component represents to the business enterprise.

The weighted average cost of capital for a small company, or subsidiary, would comprise an equity and debt rate that reflect the risk and return dynamics that are unique to the industry of the defined business enterprise. As discussed in previous chapters, the business enterprise is the sum of the fair market value of the invested capital (debt and equity). This is also represented by the sum of net working capital (monetary assets), tangible assets, and the intangible assets. Just as the weighted average cost of capital (WACOC) is allocated among the debt and equity components of the invested capital, it is also possible to allocate a portion of the WACOC to the asset components.

Weighted Average Cost of Capital				
Capital Component	Percent	Required Rate	After-tax Cost	Weighted Cost
Debt	25%	6.5%	3.9%	0.98%
Equity	75%	12.0%	12.0%	9.00%
	100%			9.98%

Weighted Average Cost of Capital					
Asset Category	Amount	Percent	Required Rate	Weighted Cost	Allocated Return
Working Capital	100	16.7%	6.5%	1.08%	10.85%
Fixed Assets	200	33.3%	9.0%	3.00%	30.05%
IA & IP	300	50.0%	11.8%	5.90%	59.10%
Total	600	100.0%		9.98%	100.00%

Shown above is an allocation of the weighted average cost of capital for a business enterprise allocated among the business assets. The various rates of return assigned to each of the assets reflect their relative risk. The relative returns provided by each asset category is also indicated.

A.5 APPROPRIATE RETURN ON MONETARY ASSETS

The monetary assets of the business are its net working capital. This is the total of current assets minus current liabilities. Current assets are comprised of accounts receivable, inventories, cash, and short term security investments. Offsetting this total are the current liabilities of the business such as accounts payable, accrued salaries, and accrued expenses. Working capital is considered to be the most liquid asset of a business. Receivables are usually collected within 60 days and inventories are usually turned over in 90 days. The cash component is immediately available and security holdings can be converted to cash with a telephone call to the firm's broker. Further evidence of liquidity is the use of accounts receivable and/or inventories as collateral for loans. In addition, accounts receivable can be sold for immediate cash to factoring companies at a discount of the book value. Given the relative liquidity of working capital, the amount of investment risk is inherently low. An appropriate rate of return to associate with the working capital component of the business enterprise is that which is available from investment in short-term securities of low risk levels.

A.6 APPROPRIATE RETURN ON TANGIBLE ASSETS

The tangible or fixed assets of the business are comprised of production machinery, warehouse equipment, transportation fleet, office buildings, office equipment, leasehold improvements, office equipment, and manufacturing plants. An indication of the rate of return that is contributed by these assets can be pegged at about the interest rate at which commercial banks make loans, using the fixed assets as collateral. While these assets are not as liquid as working capital, they can often be sold to other companies. This marketability allows a partial return of the investment in fixed assets of the business should the business fail. Another aspect of relative risk reduction relates to the strategic redeployment of fixed assets. Corporation assets that can be redirected for use elsewhere have a degree of versatility, which can still allow an economic contribution to be derived from their employment even if it isn't from the originally intended purpose. While these assets are more risky than working capital investments, they possess favorable characteristics that must be considered in the weighted average cost of capital allocation.

Fixed assets that are very specialized in nature must reflect higher levels of risk, which of course demands a higher rate of return. Specialized assets are those that are not easily redeployed for other commercial exploitation or liquidated to other businesses for other uses.

A.7   APPROPRIATE RETURN ON INTANGIBLE ASSETS AND INTELLECTUAL PROPERTY

Intangible assets are considered to be the most risky asset components of the overall business enterprise. These assets may have little, if any, liquidity and poor versatility for redeployment elsewhere in the business. This enhances their risk. Customized computer software that is installed and running on a company's computer may have very little liquidation value if the company fails. The investment in a trained work force may be altogether lost and the value of other elements of a going concern is directly related to the success of the business. A higher rate of return on these assets is therefore required. Since the overall return on the business is established as the weighted average cost of capital, and since reasonable returns for the monetary and tangible assets can be estimated, we are then in a position to derive an appropriate rate of return to be earned from the intangible assets. Equation A.6 presents the means by which the 11.8 percent rate was derived for the intangible assets and intellectual property in our example:

$$\text{WACOC} = \frac{Vm}{Vbev}(Rm) + \frac{Vt}{Vbev}(Rt) + \frac{Vi}{Vbev}(Ri) \qquad \text{(Eq. A.6)}$$

where:

WACOC is the weighted average cost of capital for the overall business enterprise.

Vm, Vt, and Vi are the fair market values of the monetary, tangible, and intangible assets respectively.

Rm, Rt, and Ri are the relative rates of return associated with the business enterprise asset components.

Vbev is the fair market value of the business enterprise, which is the total of Vm, Vt, and Vi.

If values are known or can be estimated for all but one of the afore-mentioned components, then the equation can be solved for the missing component. Typically, we are trying to find an appropriate rate of return for association with the intangible assets and intellectual property.

If the WACOC that is developed is for a diversified multinational corporation, the proper rate that should be used in conjunction with a specific intellectual property investment could be far greater. The WACOC represents an overall return from the diversified investments or asset base of the business. The rate attributed to a specific intellectual property must reflect the various risks associated with the division within which the specific property is used.

Thus, the process may first require determination of an appropriate WACOC for the whole business. Followed by a determination of a WACOC for each operating division, working toward the business segment in which a specific intellectual property resides in a "top-down" approach.

The example that was presented yielded a 9.98 percent WACOC. This was based upon use of an equity rate of return of 12 percent. Such a rate would imply that the business is commercially viable and that the associated intellectual property has also been proven. Embryonic and emerging intellectual property entail more risks and, as such, would most likely be analyzed using a venture capital rate of return.

Overall, the business enterprise is comprised of various types of assets, each possessing different degrees of investment risk that correlate with the weighted average cost of capital. An analysis can be completed for any company so that the appropriate investment rate of return can be isolated for specific intellectual property.

A.8   PREJUDGMENT INTEREST

The Federal Circuit ruled in Allen Archery, Inc. v. Browning Manufacturing Co., 898 F.2d 787, 14 USPQ2d 1156 (Fed. Cir. 1990) that infringement damages consist not only of the value of the damages awarded but also of the foregone use of the money between the time of infringement and the date of the judgment. The Federal Circuit also explained that an award of prejudgment interest is needed to ensure that the patent owner is placed in as good a position as would have been attained had the infringer initially entered into a reasonable royalty agreement. There really isn't, or at least shouldn't be, too much argument about the appropriateness of paying interest on a damage award. There is also little room to argue about the proper way of calculating the interest payment. The real argument centers on the interest rate that should be used. It is an important consideration because different interest rates can make a very significant difference in the total amount of damages.

A.9   SELECTION OF APPROPRIATE INTEREST RATES

Again, the purpose of including prejudgment interest as part of the total damage award is to place the infringed party in the same position they would have attained but for infringement. If the infringed had properly received the royalty payments or lost profits, they would have reinvested the funds and earned compound returns on the invested payments. Typically the courts have used safe investment rates of return such as that earned from investing in government securities. In Polaroid Corporation v. Eastman Kodak Co., 16 USPQ2d 1481 (D. Mass. 1990) the district court used a Treasury Bill rate for the calculation of prejudgment interest. In Sun Studs, Inc. v. ATA Equipment Leasing, Inc., 17 USPQ2d 1768 (D. Or. 1990) the district court based the prejudgment interest calculation on the short-term borrowing rate actually charged the patentee. These decisions do not necessarily place the patentee in the position that it would have otherwise attained. The proper selection of the prejudgment interest rate must consider the amount that the patentee would most likely have earned. Corporations do not invest to earn treasury security rates of return. This is an important point. Corporations invest to earn at least their weighted average cost of capital. Corporations invest to earn a fair rate of return that compensates the equity investors and the debtors of the corporation.

The amounts invested in a company come from equity shareholders and from those that provide the company with loans. Each has an expectation of the rate of return that will be earned from the different investments made. The amounts the debtors expect to earn are specified in loan agreements as the interest rate that the company must pay on the borrowed funds. The amounts equity investors expect to earn is reflected in the way they price the stock of the company. When the balanced amount of the equity and debt rates are calculated, the company must earn the weighted average cost of capital.

The total investments of a company might include some of the following types of activities:

- Construction of buildings from which to operate
- Purchase and installation of manufacturing equipment
- Funding of research and development for the introduction of better products and services
- Training programs for personnel in sales, finance, manufacturing, and operations to improve efficiency
- Payments for the development and installation of computer systems to improve the foundations of management decision making
- Development of raw material resources such as oil fields, gravel pits, or farm land

Some of the investments are also in cash accounts to serve as a buffer against bad times. Just as individuals keep funds in low interest checking accounts, corporations keep funds in various accounts that provide the liquidity needed for emergencies or sudden opportunities.

While this means that some of a company's investments might be maintained in treasury securities or checking accounts, it does not mean that the low rates of return provided by these liquid investments are the ultimate goal of the company. They are just a portion of the total goal. The total goal is to attain investment returns equaling the weighted average cost of capital. Some of this return comes from checking account interest. Some of the return comes from producing products on company machinery in company buildings. Some of the return comes from the high risk and high rewards of research and development. When these returns are all combined and balanced, the company earns the weighted average cost of capital.

When the infringed party is an individual, such as an inventor, the same principles apply. Prejudgment interest calculations should be based on an investment rate of return that would place the individual in such a position as would have been attained but for infringement. Treasury security interest rates can still be inappropriate. If the individual can show a track record of personal investment that is different from treasury rates of return, then the past investment rates of return earned by the individual from investments should prevail. An individual that has always invested in stock mutual funds could reasonably be expected to have continued such a policy had they received the royalty payments or lost profits. It can even be argued that the royalty or lost profits would have placed the individual in a position allowing for more aggressive investments with higher risk, delivering higher returns. For an individual patentee that has a track record of investing in stocks, the prejudgment interest calculation should consider the investment returns the individual would have earned from stock mutual funds. If the individual regularly stuffed money under their mattress, then a prejudgment interest calculation based on a zero rate of interest would put the patentee in the position that most likely would have been attained.

Prejudgment interest calculations must consider the investment policies, goals, investor and debtor obligations, and investment practices of the infringed party. Standardized use of treasury security interest rates for all cases is a cop-out. Such a practice is just as improper as using a standardized royalty rate of 2 percent of sales for all cases or a 40 percent incremental profit margin for lost-profit calculations. The amount of prejudgment interest comprising damages awards is becoming a substantial part of total awards. Detailed analysis should go into selecting the fairest interest rate to be used in the calculation.

REFERENCES

Cohen, Jerome B., Edward D. Zinbarg, and Arthur Zeikel. *Investment Analysis and Portfolio Management, Fourth Edition,* Homewood, Illinois: Richard D. Irwin, Inc., 1982.

Copeland, Tom, Tim Koller, and Jack Murrin (McKinsey & Company, Inc.). *Valuation: Measuring and Managing the Value of Companies*, New York: John Wiley & Sons, 1990.

Gray, William S., III. *The Historical Record: Insights for Forecasting Expected Return and Risk*, Homewood, Illinois: The Institute of Chartered Financial Analysts, Dow Jones-Irwin, 1985.

Harrington, Diana R. "Stock Prices, Beta, and Strategic Planning," *Harvard Business Review*, May–June 1983, p. 157.

Levine, Sumner N., ed. *Financial Analyst's Handbook: Portfolio Management,* Homewood, Illinois: Dow Jones-Irwin, 1975.

Maginn, John L., and Donald L. Tuttle, eds. *Managing Investment Portfolios: A Dynamic Process*, Boston: Warren, Gorham, and Lamont, 1983.

Reilly, Frank K. *Investment Analysis and Portfolio Management, Second Edition,* Chicago: The Dryden Press, 1985.

Smith, Gordon V., and Russell L. Parr. *Valuation of Intellectual Property and Intangible Assets, Second Edition,* New York: John Wiley & Sons, 1995.

APPENDIX B

Company Audit Reports Don't Show Intellectual Property

R easonable royalties and, to a certain extent, lost profits, can be looked on as a fair return from an intellectual property investment. Unfortunately, the value of the assets on which to calculate a fair return are not easy to find. Intellectual property drives the stock prices of embryonic high-tech companies. Intellectual property runs steel mills from computers. Intellectual property saves lives through advanced medical procedures. Intellectual property attracts loyal customers that recognize trusted brand names. Intellectual property is everywhere and can be argued as being the foundation of the American economy and other developed nations. Yet, in the majority of cases the most important assets that a company can own are wholly absent from the financial statements of the company.

The financial statements of a business are prepared as a medium of communication between a business entity and interested parties such as investors, suppliers, and bankers. Unfortunately, most intellectual properties aren't shown anywhere in the accounting statements, not even in a footnote. The financial statements of a business enterprise are intended to provide: (1) a "snapshot" of the assets and liabilities of the business at a specific point in time (balance sheet) and (2) a summary of the transactions of the past year (income statement).

B.1 BALANCE SHEET

The two primary elements of the balance sheet are assets and liabilities. Accounting elements that are to be included on the asset side of the balance sheet have been described as follows:

Generally Accepted Accounting Principles state that an asset has three essential characteristics: (a) it embodies a probable future benefit that involves a capacity, singly or in combination with other assets, to contribute directly or indirectly to future net cash inflows, (b) a particular entity can obtain the benefit and control others' access to it, and (c) the transaction or other event giving rise to the entity's right to or control of the benefit has already occurred. Basically, anything that is already owned by a company, lasts for more than one accounting year, directly delivers future economic benefits, and can be exclusively controlled by a business can be classified on a balance sheet as an asset. Unfortunately, this broad definition of assets is rarely utilized to the fullest extent possible, and the admirable objectives of financial statements are never fully achieved.

B.2   ACCOUNTING FOR ASSETS

The capitalization policy of fixed assets addresses the question of which expenditures should be treated as current expenses and which should be capitalized. The process of capitalization is the basis on which costs are allocated to future time periods. As an example, an expenditure for office supplies is treated as a current expense because it is reasonable to expect that the supplies will be used up within a few months or a year. It is therefore logical that the current operations of the business bear the expense. Alternatively, a building provides service to the business for a long time and it is appropriate to allocate the purchase or construction cost of the structure over a number of years. The cost of the building is therefore capitalized as an asset on the balance sheet. The mechanism for making the allocation of asset costs to accounting periods is called depreciation. In this way, there is a matching of revenues and expenses and the cost of capitalized assets is allocated over the periods in which those assets are useful to the business.

B.3 ACCOUNTING FOR INTELLECTUAL PROPERTY

Accountants have long grappled with how to treat the cost of intellectual property in financial statements. When the manager of a business makes an expenditure, it must be accounted for in some fashion. If an expenditure is used to purchase a machine, the path is clear: the cost is capitalized as an asset on the balance sheet and is depreciated (charged as an expense to income) over some period of useful life. When the expenditure is used to pay an employee, it is equally clear that it represents a payment for services rendered currently and should be accounted for as an expense of the current fiscal year. If, however, an expenditure was for research or advertising programs the answer may not be so clear. The essential question is whether the expenditure created an asset that will provide some benefit to the enterprise beyond the current period. In some cases, research expenses or advertising campaigns can be justifiably categorized as asset-creating endeavors. Narrow interpretation of accounting definitions, however, rarely allows capitalization of anything but fixed assets. Coca-Cola is one of the best-recognized trademarks in the world, but it's not on their books. The brand got its enormous recognition through advertising campaigns that have spanned a century, but because the accounting profession does not categorize advertising expenses as an asset, you won't see the COKE name on the company balance sheet.

B.4 TWO MAJOR FLAWS

The most fundamental accounting principle requires that the total value of the assets equal the total amount of liabilities plus the amount of shareholders' equity. The balance sheet relationship is expressed below:

Total Assets = Total Liabilities + Shareholders' Equity (Eq. B.1)

The absence of adequate representation of the value of intellectual property directly affects the validity of the balance sheet as follows: The absence of intellectual property understates the value of shareholders' equity. By omitting intellectual property, the accounting goal of reporting all assets that will contribute future economic benefits is not met.

B.5 MAKING MATTERS WORSE ARE ACQUISITION ACCOUNTING PRINCIPLES

The "merger mania" of the late 1980's caused a careful reexamination of the whole subject of accounting for intangible assets and intellectual property. As business executives directed resources into acquisitions, the accounting profession and the Securities and Exchange Commission were forced to face the issue in order to prevent what they perceived was a potential for misleading financial statements. Unfortunately, the results of these good intentions have provided an accounting system that is atrociously inconsistent. Internally developed trademarks, patents, copyrights, and other intangibles are not presented on balance sheets. When, as part of a corporate takeover or merger, another company acquires the exact same assets, then the intangible assets are prominently displayed on the combined balance sheet of the merged entities.

If intellectual property is self-created, it can not be shown on the financial statements of the company that created it. If another company comes along and acquires the creative company, then the intellectual property gained from the takeover can be fully incorporated onto the financial statements of the acquirer, but it depends on how the acquirer chooses to account for the acquisition. Briefly stated, an acquisition of a business enterprise can be accounted for as a "pooling of interests" or as a "purchase."

In a pooling, the recorded assets and liabilities of the companies become the recorded assets and liabilities of the combined corporation at the historical cost-basis amounts of the separate companies. The accounting values that were shown on the balance sheet of the target company before the acquisition are the same values that are absorbed into the balance sheet of the acquiring company. Intangible assets will not appear on the new balance sheet unless they were already stated on the balance sheet of the acquired company prior to the transaction. For the most part, intangible assets will not be represented when acquisitions are recorded by the pooling method.

Accounting for an acquisition treated as a purchase is similar to that of acquiring a single asset except that the price of the entire business enterprise is attributed to different asset categories. The total price for the acquisition is allocated to net working capital, fixed assets, intangible assets, and intellectual property. When an intellectual property is purchased separately from a business combination, the price is recorded as the value of the asset. When specifically identifiable intellectual property is purchased as part of a business acquisition, a portion of the total price is allocated to intellectual property and recorded on the balance sheet. Changing the decision about how to record the acquisition can mean the difference between showing or omitting intangible assets on balance sheets.

B.6   AN INCONSISTENT MESS

When an acquisition is treated as a purchase rather than a pooling, intellectual property will be placed on the balance sheet at a value represented by a portion of the price paid for the acquired business. When an acquisition is treated as a pooling of interests, intellectual property will not be identified on the opening balance sheet of the surviving company. However, if the acquired company had intellectual property prior to the merger, then the historical basis of the intellectual property will be placed on the opening balance sheet.

When a company uses funds to acquire intellectual property, independent of an on-going enterprise, the price paid for the asset will be presented on the balance sheet as the basis of the acquired independent intellectual property. When a company internally develops trademarks, patents, copyrights, and other extraordinary intellectual property the funds expended are not capitalized and intangible assets do not appear on the balance sheet.

Financial analysis has become infinitely more complicated, especially when trying to make comparisons among competitors within an industry. Some balance sheets may show intellectual property gained during an acquisition but omit intellectual property that was internally developed. Some balance sheets will not show any intellectual property at all. As the vital assets of business become more intangible, accounting statements have become less useful.

Index